THE FOURTH FORGER

Drawn from the Life & Etch'd by Silvester Harding. 1798.

W. H. Ireland
From a print in the British Museum

THE FOURTH FORGER

William Ireland and the
Shakespeare Papers

JOHN MAIR

KENNIKAT PRESS
Port Washington, N. Y./London

THE FOURTH FORGER

First published in 1938
Reissued in 1972 by Kennikat Press
Library of Congress Catalog Card No: 71-153227
ISBN 0-8046-1537-3

Manufactured by Taylor Publishing Company   Dallas, Texas

Four forgers born in one prolific age
Much critical acumen did engage
The first[1] was soon by doughty Douglas scar'd
Tho'. Johnson would have screened him had he dared
The next[2] had all the cunning of a Scot
The third,[3] invention, genius,—nay, what not?
Fraud, now exhausted, only could dispense
To her fourth son, their threefold impudence.

WILLIAM MASON, 1797

[1] Lauder   [2] Macpherson   [3] Chatterton

To
JOAN

CONTENTS

LIST OF ILLUSTRATIONS

PREFACE

The Ireland Shakespeare forgeries are unique in English literature, both for the daring of their conception and the extent of their success. For two years they were the leading literary topic, and at the height of their reputation numbered more distinguished supporters than had ever accepted the deceptions of Chatterton or Macpherson. In two respects William Ireland was far superior to his more famous predecessors. He produced his actual manuscripts and submitted them not only to his own friends, but to the supposedly expert examination of antiquarian scholars; and he was not content to discover an unknown Celtic bard or forgotten Chaucerian versifier, but presented to an astonished world the plays, poems and personal papers of the unapproachable Shakespeare. When he produced his first manuscripts, the forger was nineteen years old.

The Ireland Forgeries have been strangely neglected by historians. Numerous controversial pamphlets were published at the time, and for some years afterwards references to the Shakespeare Papers recur in journals and volumes of essays. But (if we except a brief, superficial, inaccurate little essay published at an American university) no detailed account of the deception has ever been written. The present book is an endeavour to fill the gap, and give a more complete picture of a most curious episode in the history of English letters. This neglect of the Forgeries is the more surprising since the forger himself is a highly interesting character. Had William Ireland (as he several times threatened) committed suicide after the Manuscripts were exposed, he would probably have achieved a fame equal to that of Chatterton, and his dark good looks and moody eccentricities become the theme of as many laudatory odes as celebrate his romantic predecessor. Unfortunately, he survived to become a literary hack, and oblivion rewarded the triumph of common sense.

William Ireland consciously took Chatterton as his model, and the pair had a great deal in common both of circumstance and character. Both had a craving for learning without the concentration to achieve it, both were put to the dreary routine of a lawyer's office, and in both a longing for self-expression was suppressed by an uninterested family. The naïve glee, so distressing to sentimentalists, that the Marvellous Boy took in his own lack of literary principle was a marked feature of William's character; he was capable of admiring both Lancelot and Machiavelli. The parallel between Ireland and Chatterton needed but one thing to make it perfect, and in due course the Rowley Poems found a worthy successor. How far the Shakespeare Forgeries were purely the logical outcome of a conscious identification can never certainly be determined.

William was more than a mere echo of Chatterton, and his complex personality was largely misunderstood even by his own associates. The contrasts in his nature were responsible both for the Forgeries and for the subsequent doubts of their authorship. To his own family, William Ireland seemed dull almost to idiocy, and his father makes frequent references to his silence and lack of intelligence. The easy acceptance of the Manuscripts was greatly facilitated by the supposed stupidity of their discoverer, and to the end of his life Mr. Ireland refused to believe that his son had the talent to compose the Shakespeare Papers. On the other hand, many considered William a genius, and laid particular stress on his brilliant and voluble conversation. The Forgeries themselves bear out this division of character, and show childish incompetence side by side with the most subtle and painstaking ingenuity.

When William finally confessed to the authorship of the Papers, many refused to believe him, and accused Mr. Ireland of making his son a scapegoat for his own dishonesty. William's confession was doubted until long after his death, and only his father's correspondence, here extensively quoted, has finally proved that he did, after all, speak the truth.

The Forgeries were completed before William Ireland was twenty-one, and although he lived on for another forty years he never fulfilled early expectations, but wasted the rest of his career in the precarious commonplaces of literary journalism. For a year or two he had been a genius, and expressed in himself all the brilliance and folly of his age; afterwards, he sank to the mediocrity of those who have triumphed prematurely. The Shakespeare Papers were William Ireland's unique creation; the rest of his life was the purest anticlimax.

Possessors of William Ireland's *Confessions* or his father's *Vindication* may notice that certain documents there quoted are here reproduced with differences or additions. In such cases I am quoting from the original manuscripts, before they were edited for publication. I have in no case altered the spelling or phrasing of any document, but in a number of instances I have modernised the punctuation—a necessary proceeding, since William never punctuated at all.

I am, of course, grateful to all those who in any way helped or encouraged me in the writing of this book.

Chapter One

THE IRELAND FAMILY

The Ireland family could have been called respectably Bohemian.

Samuel Ireland began life obscurely. The date and place of his birth are unknown, as are the names and condition of his parents. For a garrulous and sociable man he was surprisingly successful in concealing the details of his early years; and the statement that he started his career as a weaver at Spitalfields may as well be accepted in default of more definite evidence.

In any event, he soon bettered himself. From the inadequate evidence of a single copy-book, he seems to have been a writing-master around 1758, and also appears to have acted as tout and commission-man for a firm of engravers, in whose employ he discovered his quick imitative talents as a hack illustrator. Soon he embarked independently and built up a small but useful artistic reputation, obtaining the medal of the Society of Arts and, in 1784, exhibiting a View of Oxford at the Royal Academy. His work was pleasantly competent, and his capacity for combining perfect perspective and photographic detail into a flat, lifeless, but undeniably picturesque whole pleased the taste of the age and won him some popularity. He specialised in landscapes backed by bright, plain skies, or buildings in minute architectural detail set in pleasant surroundings, and seldom ventured on the human figure save at a safe distance as part of the scenery.

Engraving was Samuel's secondary occupation; his real

interest and profit lay in collecting. He had the mind of a cultured jackdaw; anything old, odd or rare, provided it had some historical or cultural association, excited his covetous enthusiasm, and his beloved collection included paintings by Rubens and Van Dyck, part of Wycliff's vestment, a lock of Edward IV's hair, Inigo Jones' designs for Whitehall, the seer cloth of a mummy, and Oliver Cromwell's buff leather jacket. Samuel soon found that others shared his interest in curiosities, and began a very profitable trade in books, curios and *objets d'art.*

The middle of the eighteenth century was the heyday of the antique dealer. Trade had been widely profitable long enough for its followers to have become gentlefolk and their servants to have assumed the dignities and pretensions of professional men. Increasing prosperity gave the middle class the time and means to imitate the cultured affectations of the nobility; and led, as usual, by George III, the bourgeoisie developed an eager interest in the antique. Astute taste and a flair for business had every opportunity, and such a man as James Lackington, who began by selling pies on the streets and ended as proprietor of the biggest bookshop in the country with "half a million volumes constantly on sale," was by no means an exceptional figure.

Samuel's business was not on the scale of Lackington's, but it was profitable enough, and of a rather higher social standing. Buying cheap from the spendthrift heirs of noble houses, or still cheaper from the stalls and junk shops round the Strand and Chancery Lane, he sold at a handsome profit to the new dilettante, or added another rarity to his own collection. Business led him to great houses and made him influential connections, and an association that began in trade often ended in a gratifying friendship, and helped the growth of an already comfortable income.

In 1789 Samuel was encouraged to a new venture, and published *A Picturesque Tour through Holland, Brabant and Part of France* in two handsome volumes dedicated to Francis Grose, Burns' debauched and antiquarian friend. The book gave a pleasantly polished and insular account of the customs and antiquities of the places visited, enlivened by congratulatory remarks on the fall of the Bastille, and a discreet description, inserted probably for Grose's benefit, of a visit to an Antwerp brothel. The volumes were plentifully illustrated with engravings in the author's best style and achieved an immediate success. In the following years Samuel published similar accounts of the Thames and the Medway, and moved to a larger and more comfortable house in Norfolk Street, Strand.

There was another side to Samuel's character. His instincts, writings and social behaviour were those of a conventional and respected gentleman, but behind his prim façade he concealed a capacity for simple and straightforward sharp-practice. In 1787, for instance, Walpole, writing to the Countess of Ossory, remarks in reference to a pamphlet of which he had produced an edition of forty copies, that "a Mr. Ireland, a collector (I believe with interested views), bribed my engraver to sell him a print of the frontispiece, has etched it himself, and I have heard, has reprinted the piece . . . and I suppose will sell some copies as part of the forty." Again, there was the affair of the Hogarths. Samuel was a great admirer of Hogarth, of whose work he had gathered a very fine collection, and in 1794 published *Graphic Illustrations of Hogarth, from Pictures, Drawings, and scarce Prints in the Author's possession.* It was alleged by his enemies that some of the Hogarths were spurious, being the work of other lesser artists or even of Ireland himself. They were unable to offer conclusive proof of their allegations, but it must be admitted that some of the prints look dubious enough to justify some suspicion. It seems curious, to say the least, that a man of Samuel's acknowledged authority should not have published with more discretion.

Even assuming the worst in both cases, there are no real grounds for regarding Samuel as a professional swindler. Whatever his motives in the Strawberry Hill pirating, gain can have played no important part. Walpole's edition, as everyone knew, was limited to forty copies; it would have been impossible for a forger to dispose of more than half this number, and, at the published price, very difficult for him even to cover his expenses. If Walpole's allegation, for which there is no other evidence, is true, it is quite possible that Samuel meant not to swindle but merely to add to his collection. Strawberry Hill pamphlets, especially in such small editions, were very hard to come by even at the time of publication, and it may be that Samuel, unable to obtain copies for a friend or for his own collection, decided to reproduce them himself. The eighteenth-century collector was not as particular as his descendants; he allowed degrees of authenticity.

The deception, if deception it was, in regard to the Hogarths, looks very unlike an intentional fraud. Samuel made no attempt to dispose of the originals, and can have got no profit by publishing a few dubious prints amidst a mass of genuine rarities. Much the most probable explanation is in a childish enthusiasm for his collection that made wish compel belief, and hope take the place of criticism. Malicious rivals alleged deliberate fraud, and could not or would not see the fundamental difference between self-deception and the deliberate deceiving of others. At the time Samuel's naïve unscrupulousness did him no harm; later he was to pay for it.

By the 1790's, in his early middle age, the plump, pert little Polonius of a man was well established, and his house by the river was the centre of a pleasantly cultivated social life, in which his own taste and an old association with Thomas Linley, part owner of the Drury Lane, brought him into contact with a stimulating circle of actors, dramatists, and all the faintly disreputable hangers-on of a great theatre. Business, too, became steadily more prosperous, and the rich dilettante and fashionable literateur dined under his roof to appraise, admire and perhaps be allowed to purchase the rare prints and curious tracts that adorned his walls and packed his bookshelves. For his enemies to call his house a shop was merely to betray their own vulgarity.

Samuel's household was as irreproachable as his profession. His wife had died before he attained his modest distinction, but his own comfort and the care of his children was capably looked after by his housekeeper, Mrs. Freeman, an educated and efficient woman, whose deep admiration for Samuel did not prevent her ruling him and his family with a discreet but firm control. Mrs. Ireland had possessed modest but entertaining literary talents, and went into print on at least one occasion with a rhyming attack on Dr. Cadogan, who had been so absurd as to prescribe outdoor exercise and abstinence from spirits as a cure for gout. There seems to have been some secret about the marriage, for neither Samuel nor his son have left any record concerning it. But perhaps that was only the influence of Mrs. Freeman.

When he moved to Norfolk Street, Samuel had three surviving children. The eldest, Anna Maria, was married, and lived with her husband at Greenwich, but the two younger, Jane and William Henry, stayed quietly at home with their father. Both the girls had some artistic talent, and Samuel directed their work into tasteful and restrained forms, encouraging Anna Maria to attempt a large oil painting of Locke, while her younger sister was allowed the more girlish self-expression of painting miniatures, usually of Milton, Dryden and other suitable poets. The sisters were both talented and obedient; their brother William Henry, while possibly the first, was certainly not the second.

Although Samuel had many literary and dramatic acquaintances at a time when the Muses kept pretty disorderly company, his own home life was a model of respectable discretion. Without being a disciplinarian he kept his children well in order; they might enjoy frequent visits to the play and have the run of the backstage at Drury Lane, but the family dined quietly at home five nights out of seven. Here, undisturbed, in his own house, Samuel could indulge his obsessing interest—the reading, study and discussion of Shakespeare.

Samuel had long admired Shakespeare, and was always ready to cap an opinion or prove a point by an apt and telling quotation from the Plays or Sonnets. As he grew older and more settled, and the shifts and ardours of his work the less intensely preoccupying, his interest in Shakespeare became a hobby, and the hobby a dominating mania. Almost invariably after a family dinner Samuel would ominously shift the chairs into a circle and organise a dramatic reading from one of the plays, with himself in the leading part, and the other characters allotted appropriately to Mrs. Freeman and the children. After the reading they would discuss the plot, poetry and meaning of the play until bedtime, with Samuel endlessly praising the poet's dramatic genius, sighing over the mystery that shrouded his life, and continually repeating that he would give all his curious books for but one line from the Master's pen. At first William was impatient of this continual adulation, but gradually he caught his father's enthusiasm, until the glory of Shakespeare fired his ambition and inflamed his imagination. Samuel never could foresee the consequence of his own actions.

William Henry Ireland was born the second of twins and named after St. John Bolingbroke, for whom his father had then a great admiration. The elder of the brothers had been honoured with the name of Samuel, but he died while William was still a child, and Mr. Ireland, who set great store on the perpetuation of his own name, habitually called his surviving son Sam. The circumstances of William's birth are somewhat obscure. According to his father, he was born in 1775, a date for which there is inferential support in one of William's letters; but his own account, which has been generally accepted, puts his birth two years later. The earlier date is probably correct; William was highly inaccurate over detail, and often tried to exaggerate his already remarkable precocity. There was certainly something a little mysterious about his parentage. The malicious Malone alleges that he was baptised W. H. Irwyn, and was the illegitimate son of a married woman with whom Samuel was living. There appears to be no evidence for such a statement, but William himself had doubts of his own legitimacy, and sometimes suspected that Mrs. Freeman might be his mother. Samuel was fond of hinting at portentous secrets that must one day be revealed, and shadowy queries about his own identity may have had the profoundest effect on William's psychological development.

In later life William used to boast of his extraordinary dullness as a child, and relates with unwarranted pride that Mr. Shury, the Usher of Ealing, refused to keep him as his pupil, declaring that his laziness and stupidity made his continued presence an injury to the school's reputation and his father's pocket. The boy's aptitudes were never scholastic, and for many years he spelt by ear, completely omitted punctuation and lost his head in long sentences, while his literary and historical knowledge was wild and inaccurate in the extreme. His chief interest was in the stage, and the happiest of his holidays were spent behind the scenes of Drury Lane, as his working hours were most enjoyably employed in the surreptitious manufacture of cardboard theatres.

He never forgot the dramatic glories of his childhood: the first nights at the play, or an end-of-term production of *Lear* at Dr. Barrow's Academy in Soho Square. The high-light of his childish memories was the wonderful day at Sheridan's house in Bruton Street, when he played in a children's performance of *The Gentle Shepherd* before "a large party of the nobility." A quarter of a century later William remarks of the occasion, "My character, though of a trivial nature, did not diminish the zest I felt on that occasion; but, on the contrary, rendered my predilection for theatrical pursuits even more determined." The eager, pale, nervous child of twelve or so, forgetting his shyness and day-dreams in the glamour of candle-lit pretence and the exhilaration of public applause, can hardly have thought of it quite like that; he had tasted flattering recognition for the first time and was never to forget it.

About this time William's weakness and delicacy began to alarm his father, who resolved to send him away to a healthy part of the country. As an ordinary school was simply a waste of money, it seemed best to put him abroad, where even the laziest pupil must at least learn the language. The triumph of the Revolution and the success of his first book had filled Samuel with admiration for the French, and made France the obvious choice. William remained for four years on the Continent, first at Amiens and later at the college of Eu in Normandy, where he acquired revolutionary sentiments and a thorough knowledge of the language which he was later to find very useful. He seems to have been happy in France, perhaps because he was free from his father's continual cold water. But the time came to return home and face the dreaded necessity of entering a profession. Samuel sadly noted his son's lack of useful talents, complete indifference to sensible ambitions, and obvious inclination for the life of a cultivated waster. Something had to be done with William, and so, near his seventeenth birthday, he was put to study law under Mr. Bingley, a conveyancer of New Inn. No choice could have proved more unfortunate.

William's was a highly romantic and introspective nature. At first, influenced by Chaucer and the Percy Reliques, he was obsessed by the Medieval, and longed to be a knight-errant, doing terrible deeds on gloomy heaths, or finding "the hospitable porch of some old monastery where, with the holy brotherhood, having shared at the board their homely fare, I might afterwards have enjoyed upon the pallet a sound repose, and, with the Abbot's blessing the ensuing morn, have hied me in pursuit of fresh adventures." These were the ordinary adolescent day-dreams of the period, but William went further than most boys, and tried to re-create his romances in real life, buying old pieces of armour, polishing them till the metal gleamed, and making up incomplete suits with strips of cardboard. As the moonlight streamed in on the shining, faceless figures around his bed, he would sit up staring, his head swirling with visions of the feudal North and the Gothic horrors of the Castle of Otranto.

But William never really imagined himself as a knight-errant; even in his Chaucerian period he affected the poet rather than one of his characters, and found his greatest pleasure in imitating medieval verse.

> *Can I yn rythms thilke clerks fame make knowen*
> *Hondlynge so poorlee thys my quille*
> *As rathere makes me hys fame kille . . .*

he asks, with patently false modesty, and proceeds with a lumbering acrostic in praise of Chaucer whom he continued to admire all his life. Perhaps, he thought, his true vocation was the poetic; that would explain his dislike of his work, unhealthy pallor and half-contempt for his father's learned propriety. While William still searched in himself for authentic evidence of the divine fire, Samuel quite unconsciously provided the ideal model. The evening readings were not always Shakespearian, and on one of these occasions Mr. Ireland read extracts from Sir Herbert Croft's highly entertaining *Love and Madness*, choosing, unfortunately, the letters relating to

Chatterton. William was enormously impressed. The poet's youth, romantic appearance, brilliant beginning and tragic suicide seemed all reflected in his own personality, and he became convinced that he was another Chatterton in genius and in doom. "The fate of Chatterton," he afterwards wrote, "so strongly interested me, that I used frequently to envy his fate, and desire nothing so ardently as the termination of my existence in a similar cause." He took to writing acrostics and ballads, affected a more mercurial temperament even than he possessed, and pathetically attempted to bring his poetry to his father's notice.

But Samuel was quite oblivious of his son's genius, and dismissed with kindly condescension the poems he timidly presented. His antiquarian interests gave him a contempt for modern literature, and he suffered from the delusion, common to lovers of the antique, that age alone can sanction the æsthetic. In his heart of hearts, he regarded all present and future poetry as foredoomed to mediocrity for the vice of having been born too late; where his son was concerned he stated his belief openly. Any lingering interest he might have felt in William's work was crushed by Mrs. Freeman. With the righteous intolerance peculiar to the semi-cultured woman, she knew what she liked, and what she didn't know she despised. She regarded William with a mixture of spiteful jealousy and honest contempt, and hated him as much for disobeying Samuel as for winning his affection. His romantic ambitions gave magnificent opportunity for working off all her varied feelings at the same time, and she never lost an opening for jeering at his pretensions before his face or behind his back. Praise and recognition were essential to William's happiness, and the admiration of his sister Jane was poor compensation for his learned father's scarcely veiled contempt. Something else had to be done.

In one respect William won his father's whole-hearted approval. Samuel's antiquarian enthusiasm, and the atmosphere of musty learning that prevailed in Mr. Bingley's office, early encouraged William's taste for collecting, and soon, with the aid of a quick memory for his father's observations, and a good deal of time borrowed from the office in his employer's absence, he acquired from the stalls and shops round the Temple a collection of old books rare enough to excite the admiration of Samuel and his friends. If Samuel was unfeeling over literary talent, he was highly interested in the antique, and gave his son unstinted praise and encouragement for his new interest, so that even Mrs. Freeman had to add her grudging approval. But in spite of this welcome recognition William was not satisfied; collecting was an important hobby, but his real ambitions were creative. If only the two could be combined—anything written 200 years ago was sure of his father's approbation. Chatterton had discovered the same truth, and though the Rowley Poems were unmasked, they had given their inventor a deathless glory. William read and thought on Chatterton, and realised ever more clearly that they had much in common. Who can mark exactly the transition of wish into idea, and idea into determination?

Chapter Two

THE JOURNEY TO STRATFORD

In the spring of 1793 Samuel Ireland decided to follow up his *Picturesque Views of the River Medway* with a similar volume on the Warwickshire Avon, and, accompanied by his son, set out on a tour to gather material and make sketches for his intended book. For a time he followed his usual course of questioning innkeepers, visiting the local gentry, and making appropriate drawings of picturesque prospects; but arriving at Stratford itself, the very place of his idol's birth and death, he abandoned business, and gave himself up to an orgy of worship and research, filling William's impressionable mind with "a thousand little anecdotes and surmises respecting the sub-lunary career of our dramatic lord."

Samuel had opportunity enough to indulge in adulation, for by this time Shakespeare-worship had become culture's commonplace and Stratford's most prosperous industry.

There were a good many reasons for the age to take Shakespeare to its heart. In the first place he was a dramatist, and in the eighteenth century the dramatic was easily the most popular of the arts. Most county towns had their own theatres, and touring repertory companies brought acting of a high standard even to the outlying districts of Devonshire and Wales. Except amongst certain sections of the Dissenters, the Play was quite respectable, although actors were still held in ill-repute by the more solid of the middle classes; and we find a respectable country clergyman such as Parson Woodforde travelling quite long distances to see visiting players in the latest farce. The age was still close enough to Shakespeare in spirit to appreciate his plays for their own sake, but far enough away in time to regard his genius with the uncritical respect reserved for antiquity. Shakespeare, too, was morally and socially highly admirable. He was reasonably free from the deplorable grossness so common in the ancients, he expressed no opinions that were certainly his own, displayed no eccentric affectations of style, and could be just disrespectful enough to the established orders to amuse without giving offence. Finally, practically nothing was known of his life except that he made money, bought a great house and died respected by his neighbours. He showed an admirable combination of immense talent and complete freedom from Enthusiasm; he made, in fact, the ideal bourgeois hero.

Stratford was the natural focus of this growing interest, and in 1769 Garrick set the seal on the town's reputation by organising a great Shakespeare Jubilee. The Stratford Jubilee was the most fashionable event of the year, and the greater part of London society crowded up to the little town for the fêtes, banquets and celebrations. The Corporation played up well to the occasion, and built a great, octagonal, semi-Corinthian amphitheatre on the banks of the Avon, where, amidst the elegant gildings and beneath the blazing light of 800 candles set in a huge chandelier, the visitors dined for 10s. 6d. a head (claret and madeira included), or danced through the night in Shakespearian fancy-dress.

The first day of the festivities was given over to serenades, oratorios, and the singing of popular songs written by Garrick. The most popular of these was *The Warwickshire Lad*, and the

fashionable company sang with great enthusiasm seven such
verses as:

> *Old Ben, Thomas Otway, John Dryden*
> *And half-a-score more we take pride in;*
> *Of famous Will Congreve we boast too the skill,*
> **But the Will of all Wills was a Warwickshire Will**
> > *Warwickshire Will*
> > *Matchless still*
> *But the Will of all Wills was a Warwickshire Will. . . .*

which at least one hearer found "absolutely inspiring." On the
second day Garrick dedicated the new Town Hall. The building had been decorated for the occasion with transparent
paintings of Lear, Falstaff, Pistol, Caliban, and Time leading
Shakespeare to Immortality, and the dedication and unveiling
of the Bard's statue were performed with the most moving
ceremony. "The performance of the Dedication Ode," wrote
Boswell, "was noble and affecting; it was like an exhibition in
Athens or Rome. The whole audience were fixed in the most
earnest attention; and I do believe, that if one had attempted
to disturb the performance, he would have been in danger of
his life. Garrick, in the front of the orchestra, filled with the
first musicians of the nation, with Dr. Arne at their head, and
inspired with an awful elevation of soul, while he looked from
time to time at the venerable statue of Shakespeare, appeared
more than himself. While he repeated the Ode, and saw the
various passions and feelings which it contains fully transfused
into all around him, he seemed in ecstasy, and gave us the idea
of a mortal transformed into a demigod, as we read in the
pagan mythology." The following day was not such a success,
and torrential rain spoilt the procession of Shakespearian

Characters. But the evening's masquerade was attended by 2,000 people.

The townsfolk, at first uncertain of what the fuss was about, soon awoke to its possibilities, as one visitor observed:

> *To bed I must go—for which like a ninny*
> *I paid—like my betters—no less than a guinea,*
> *For rolling—not sleeping—in linen so damp*
> *As struck my great toe ever since with the cramp.*

The relic dealers profited also, and Shakespeare's mulberry-tree was marvellously multiplied to provide mementos for the curious enthusiast. Stratford never looked back from this splendid start, and by the time of Samuel's visit the town had already assumed the air of commercial reverence it wears to-day.

If Samuel and his son wanted Shakespearian anecdote and surmise, they found the perfect guide in John Jordan, the Stratford poet. Jordan was a curious creature. Born of a working-class family and brought up to be a wheelwright, he possessed a deep and muddled enthusiasm for history and the arts without the education or abilities to perfect himself in either. The Stratford Jubilee stirred his ambitions, and he presented Garrick with a poetical address of unparalleled dullness and mediocrity, following up this attempt eight years later with an historical poem based on the legends surrounding Welcombe Hills near Stratford. But his poetry was not a success, and he soon found that Shakespeare offered him far the greater possibilities. A bad poet was of no interest, but a literary rustic with a folk-knowledge of Shakespeare appealed

to the researcher in everyone, and Jordan's Shakespearian Anecdotes and Traditions, some of them probably quite genuine,
found their way into the note-books and memoirs of a good
many visitors. With his dark, heavy face, fuzzy black hair and
ploughman's physique, Jordan gave a deceptive impression of
honest stupidity, and William condescendingly describes him as
"an honest fellow" and a "civil inoffensive creature." Actually,
he was a quick-witted romancer with an extraordinary gift of
judging exactly how much each enquirer would swallow. He
imposed on Samuel as thoroughly as on much more sceptical
predecessors.

Under Jordan's able leadership the pair toured the town and
paid their homage to Shakespeare's living memory. Samuel, of
course, eagerly sought material relics of the Bard, visited Mr.
Sharpe, an old shopkeeper who possessed the remains of the
famous mulberry-tree, and bought "for an adequate price" a
cup and other curios made from the sacred wood. At Shottery,
Ann Hathaway's village, he had even greater good fortune, and
was permitted to purchase a bugle purse given by Shakespeare
during his courting, and the very oak chair in which the poet
used to sit holding Ann upon his knee. Jordan, too, did his
best to entertain Mr. Ireland, and, for a small consideration,
wrote out a traditional anecdote of Shakespeare's drinking
exploits, together with a song the poet sang under a crab-tree
on the morning after. With such good fortune Samuel's
enthusiasm passed all bounds, and his talk from breakfast to
supper was continually of Shakespeare and his genius.

Although greatly encouraged by these relics, Samuel was not
satisfied; his real ambition was to discoverer fresh literary
evidence on Shakespeare's life and work. Here Jordan was of

little help, but at length, under ceaseless questioning, some of the oldest inhabitants remembered a tradition that, at the time of the Stratford Fire, bundles of manuscripts had been carried away for safety from New Place to Clopton House, a Tudor manor about a mile from the town, now owned by one Williams, a gentleman farmer.

The house itself was highly picturesque, and its gabled complexity, low passages and dark untidy rooms seemed to promise every kind of discovery. But if his house was inviting, Mr. Williams was not, and he and the Irelands seem to have taken an immediate dislike to each other. William describes their host as "rich in gold and the worldly means of accumulating wealth, but devoid of every polished refinement," while for his part he seems to have regarded the pair as ridiculous antiquaries and a perfect target for practical joking. When Samuel, with what eager pedantry can be imagined, asked if he had any papers relating to Shakespeare, Williams remembered some immediately.

"By God," he exclaimed, "I wish you had arrived a little sooner! Why, it isn't a fortnight since I destroyed several basketsful of letters and papers, in order to clear a small chamber for some young partridges which I wished to bring up alive: and as for Shakespeare, why, there were many bundles with his name wrote upon them. Why, it was in this very fire-place I made a roaring bonfire of them."

Samuel was overwhelmed with horror and started from his chair.

"My God," he cried, clasping his hands in anguish, "Sir, you are not aware of the loss which the world has sustained. Would to heaven I had arrived sooner!"

Delighted with the success of his story Mr. Williams called his wife, who entered as quickly as if she had been listening outside the door.

"My dear," he asked, "don't you remember bringing me down those baskets of papers from the partridge room? And that I told you there were some about Shakespeare the poet?"

"Yes, my dear," she answered at once, "I do remember it perfectly well and, if you will call to mind my words, I told you not to burn the papers as they might be of consequence."

Evidently Mrs. Williams was used to her husband.

Samuel pulled himself together and searched the house for some hours, but nothing beside the partridges did he discover. Williams, perhaps moved to repentance by his guest's desolation, contemptuously presented him with an illuminated picture on vellum of Elizabeth of York lying in state, remarking that he gave it as "a picture which was in his opinion of no service, because, being on vellum, it would not do to light the fire."

Williams was punished for his imagination. In November of the same year Jordan in a letter to Samuel says, "he would have wrote to you himself but he is so averse to scribbling that he almost dreads the thought of putting pen to paper, but says he will set to work in a short time and write you a very long letter . . . he was rather out of temper about the papers he told us he had destroyed, for Mr. Malone from the information I had given him on the subject wrote to Mr. Wyatt [Williams' landlord], in which letter he observed to Mr. Wyatt that he did not see what business a tenant had to destroy his landlord's papers. Mr. Williams endeavoured to excuse himself of the indiscretion, and said that Mr. Wyatt had all the Clopton papers away . . . and said the affair was nothing to nobody, neither did he care about it. . . ."

Apparently Williams never set to work to write to Samuel, and, in spite of his denials, the story of the unfortunate bonfire persisted into the middle of the next century.

Samuel returned to London with his enthusiasm as inflamed as his search was unrewarded. His experience at Clopton House encouraged rather than depressed him; the very casualness with which the papers had been destroyed offered hope of an equally casual discovery, and he never ceased to remind his son that Shakespeare's signature alone would be worth more to him than anything else in the world.

On William, Stratford had had rather a different effect. Like his father he returned with increased enthusiasm for the poet; but, as the sight of Shakespeare's actual birthplace and all the fresh relics of his everyday life quickened his interest in the man, so, at the same time, they brought back his sense of proportion. In spite of Samuel's windy panegyrics the poet was only a human being, if one of extraordinary genius, subject to all the accidents of everyday life; he was a hero to be admired and imitated, not a god to be distantly worshipped. Shakespeare, in fact, had ceased to be an æsthetic principle that William accepted out of convention, and become a real person to be revered and even copied. By usurping the centre of William's imagination he had come within the range of his boundless self-conceit.

As William's admiration for Shakespeare increased, his

respect for Samuel diminished. He must have been astonished at the ease with which his cultured father was duped and swindled by the crude wiles of local shopkeepers and the absurd stories of Jordan and his friends. With all his romantic daydreams and luxuriant imaginings William had a central hardness that his father lacked, and, since he still regarded Samuel as an immensely superior person, he began, like many intelligent children, to assume not that his father was exceptionally gullible, but that he himself was much more astute than the general run of people. What Stratford swindlers could do he could do also, and if he could deceive Samuel he could deceive anyone. It was· not long before he began to act on his conclusions.

New Inn seemed very dull after the Avon. When first William was articled Mr. Bingley had kept a hackney-writer constantly employed in his chambers, but some months afterwards the man was dismissed, and William was left alone in the office for the greater part of the day, with freedom from supervision as the only compensation for boredom. In the mornings, on his way to the empty office, he would stroll round the bookstalls searching for Shakespeariana with ever-decreasing hope, and perhaps pick up for a few pence some curious tract to amuse his day and enlarge his collection. On one of these occasions he bought a small quarto volume of prayers, dedicated to Queen Elizabeth and adorned with elaborate woodcut borders. The volume was beautifully bound in vellum stamped with the Queen's arms, and this, coupled with the dedication, suggested that it might be a presentation copy from the author to his Patroness. This, partly as an idle test of skill, William determined to establish, and, weakening ink with water to give an appearance of age, wrote on an old piece of parchment from the piles that littered the office a letter of presentation from the author to Queen Elizabeth.

On his way home that afternoon he called on Laurie, his bookbinder, and showed him the letter, saying he had just written it and intended to try how far Mr. Ireland would credit it. Mr. Laurie was much impressed by its appearance, but one of his journeymen remarked that the ink looked too modern, and thereupon made William a mixture of three marbling fluids that wrote faintly but dried in a few minutes to a deep faded brown. William went back to his office and copied out the letter again with the new ink, inserting the completed imitation between the cover of the book and a loose end-paper. That evening he showed it to Samuel, who examined it carefully, pronounced it genuine, and urged his son to be encouraged by such good fortune to pursue his search for even greater treasures, repeating for the hundredth time the wonderful possibility of discovering a document relating to Shakespeare himself.

In a way Samuel was bound to accept this first forgery. He had no reason at all to suspect William, who had previously discovered rarities of equal interest; the book itself was certainly genuine and may actually have been a presentation copy, while the letter, with its old parchment, faded ink and half-illegible handwriting, must have appeared superficially convincing even to an expert. I have found no further trace of the book beyond William's description of its discovery, and, with its accompanying letter, it is quite probably the pride of some distinguished collection. Samuel should, perhaps, have asked how the Queen came to insert such a letter behind the end-paper of a book presented to her. But that sort of question never occurred to him; it would have been deserting scholarship for common sense.

This first success encouraged William immensely. His father had urged him to discover Shakespearian manuscripts, and he determined to follow his advice. But this time the forgery was too important to be conceived and executed in an afternoon, and he settled down to careful study and preparation.

Chapter Three

THE FIRST FORGERIES

The first forgery was moderately conceived and impeccably executed. At this time William's sole idea was to please his father by discovering a document bearing Shakespeare's signature; he had no intention of attempting a public fraud, or of essaying to copy more than the poet's handwriting. The surest means of establishing a signature was to affix it to a legal document; and William, copying the heads of the Blackfriars mortgage deed from a facsimile in Johnson's Shakespeare, drew up a lease between William Shakespeare and John Heming, and Michael Fraser and Elizabeth, his wife. In his initial effort he attempted no originality, but slavishly followed his model in language and spelling, even choosing Blackfriars for the locality of the property leased. So far from rousing suspicion, the close similarity between the two deeds passed almost unnoticed, or even helped to substantiate the authenticity of the second.

From the beginning William took care over technical details. Searching through the Elizabethan and Jacobean documents that filled Mr. Bingley's office, he cut off the blank end of a seventeenth-century rent-roll, and wrote out the Lease in the faded ink he had used for his first forgery, carefully copying Shakespeare's signature from a tracing of the facsimile in the Commons. The chief difficulty was to affix the seals, which in Jacobean times had been stamped in hot wax on to strips of parchment pendent from the deed immediately under the signature. It was obviously impossible to use modern wax, and when William tried to heat old seals in a shovel, the dried wax cracked and crumbled but would not melt. At last it occurred to him to split an old seal down the middle with a knife, scrape a cavity in the inside of the blank half, and fix in the parchment with modern wax, finally rubbing the seal with soot and ash to conceal the join. He had chosen in the first place a seal with an almost illegible device, and he saw with satisfaction that this final treatment made deciphering absolutely impossible. Much later, a visitor dropped the Lease, and the seal split down the join. But William picked it up and tied it together with silk thread before anyone could examine the inside of the wax, and later made assurance more certain by re-sealing the broken halves, so that even had the thread been untied the searcher would have found the seal miraculously whole. Taken purely as a piece of craftsmanship, the Lease was a really admirable beginning.

William's real problem was not the execution of the forgeries but the explanation of their discovery. His father's first enquiry would be for the source of this wonderful find, and it might have proved difficult to pretend it had been made in some actual shop or stall. There was also another reason for a less obvious story. In spite of the strong affirmations he afterwards made in his *Confessions*, it is difficult to believe that William really intended to stop at his first imposture, and that only its enormous success induced him, half against his will, to continue the forgeries. He certainly never anticipated the warmth of his reception, but it seems almost certain that he intended to continue forging at least on a small scale for the benefit of his father, and for that reason it was essential to name some source beyond Samuel's investigation from which further documents might be produced. As it happened, this second deception assumed nearly the importance of the first, and finally became almost an end in itself.

On December 2nd, 1794, he first broke the news to his father. On November 22nd, alleged William, he had dined at the house of Samuel's acquaintance, Mr. Mitchell the banker, where, among other company, he had met a Gentleman of considerable property. Finding him interested in old books, the Gentleman had invited William to come to his chambers where there were many old papers that had been in his family for 150 years, saying that he could look them over and keep for himself any he found of interest. After a fortnight's delay he had called on the Gentleman, who chid him for his tardiness, and told him to look through a great chest of manuscripts that stood at the back of the room. A few minutes afterwards he found the Lease. "This Deed," noted Samuel in his daybook of the discoveries, "he handed over to the Gent. who was sitting by the fire reading, and speaking of his discovery with a degree of ecstasy, the Gent. looked at it and said, 'Is this the thing that pleases you?' to which he replying in the affirmative, the Gent. gave it into his hand and said, 'You are very welcome to it, and to anything else of the kind that you meet with. . . .' " But the Gent. had added two provisos to his generosity, first, that the Deed should not be taken away until he had examined it carefully, which would not be for ten days as he had business at his country house, and secondly, that William should swear never to reveal his name, address or identity. To both these conditions William had willingly assented.

Whether to summon up courage, or whether to enjoy as long as possible the unfamiliar warmth of his father's respect and deference, William waited a fortnight before producing the

Lease. On December 16th, in the evening before dinner, he presented it to Samuel before the whole family. Ten years afterwards the details of the presentation were still vivid in his mind; amidst the muddled afterthoughts of his *Confessions* the scene stands out like a photograph.

"There, Sir! What do you think of that?" Mr. Ireland, opening the parchment, regarded it for a length of time with the strictest scrutiny: he then examined the seals; and afterwards proceeded to fold up the instrument; and on presenting it to me he replied—"I certainly believe it to be a genuine deed of the time." Returning it immediately into Mr. Ireland's hand, I then made answer—"If you think so, I beg your acceptance of it." Mr. Ireland, immediately taking the keys of his library from his pocket, presented them to me, saying—"It is impossible for me to express the pleasure you have given me by the presentation of this deed: there are the keys of my bookcase; go and take from it whatsoever you please; I shall refuse you nothing." I instantly returned the keys into Mr. Ireland's hand, saying—"I thank you, Sir; but I shall accept of nothing." Mr. Ireland, rising from his chair, selected from his books a scarce tract, with engraved plates, called *Stokes the Vaulting Master*,[1] which he peremptorily insisted I should accept. . . .

At last William had really attracted his father's attention.

On Thursday, after a day's examination had convinced him that the Deed was genuine, Samuel took it to the Heralds' Office to identify the seals. But the Heralds, although enviously

[1] William was not quite accurate here. The book was really *The Vaulting Master* by William Stokes, published in 1652. Samuel had it priced at £3 3s. 0d., which means he considered it of considerable value, since he charged a guinea less for a Second Folio. Even so, it hardly seems a fair swop for a document signed by Shakespeare.

convinced of its authenticity, were unable to decipher the least device on the cracked and grimy wax of two hundred years. Someone more expert and intelligent was required, and Samuel wrote to his friend Sir Frederick Eden.

Sir Frederick was an active and talented young man. In his short life he founded the Globe Insurance Company, wrote, at the age of thirty-one, a treatise on economics that led Marx to describe him as "the only disciple of Adam Smith during the eighteenth century that produced any work of importance," was the author of several witty poems, and acquired a valuable collection of books and antiques. Besides these major activities he fancied himself expert on a good many subjects, amongst them the reading and identification of ancient seals, and if his knowledge on such matters was not quite equal to his skill as an economist, his brilliance and enthusiasm were more than compensation. On Saturday morning he called on Samuel, full of excitement and eager to see the Deed, whose appearance immediately convinced him of its genuineness. But he had come as an expert, not as an admirer, and gave all his attention to deciphering Shakespeare's seal. Before long he detected a figure in the dirt of the crumbled surface and "looking at it with care and attention, he said he *thought* it was the Quintain—and a few minutes afterwards *decidedly* pronounced it to be so." Much excited, the pair referred to a drawing of a quintain in Stow's *Survey of London,* and found it, according to Sir Frederick, exactly similar to the shape he had found on the seal. What object could have been more suitable for the seal of punning Shakespeare? Sir Frederick, at any rate, was ardently convinced of the importance of his discovery, and urgently but unsuccessfully pressed his host to exchange the Lease for several rare books. From that time the quintain was generally accepted as Shakespeare's device, and in the facsimile of the Lease that Samuel afterwards had made, it stands out on the seal plainly and unmistakably. Sir Frederick was but the first of a long series of experts who saw, or thought they saw, or for their credit's sake pretended to see, proofs of the authenticity of the papers as far past William's knowledge to imagine, as they would have been beyond his skill to fabricate.

The ease with which the Lease had deceived his father urged William to attempt another forgery while Samuel's enthusiasm remained at white heat. He still lacked courage to venture beyond legal formalities, contenting himself with a Note of Hand from Shakespeare to Heming, promising him five guineas at the end of the month, and to prove the poet's promptness and honesty, he added Heming's receipt of the payment dated exactly a month later. The style was formal and impersonal, the spelling modern, apart from the addition of an occasional "e" or the substitution of "y" for "i," and the letters found in Shakespeare's signature were reproduced as frequently as possible in the text. There is little wonder that Samuel accepted it with the same alacrity as he had accepted its predecessor.

Two days later William produced his first major composition. A friend of Samuel's unconsciously suggested the subject by mentioning Southampton's supposed patronage of the poet, and regretting the lack of evidence for such noble and generous recognition, which would have proved Shakespeare a respectable writer, admired by court and society. This evidence William decided to supply, and in an afternoon at the office wrote the poet's letter of thanks to his patron, and Southampton's friendly and courteous reply. For fear that exact details might afterwards be discovered, he was careful to omit the precise facts of the patronage, but in the mistaken belief that no specimens of Southampton's handwriting were still in existence, he scrawled his letter almost illegibly with the left hand, merely endeavouring to make the writing as different as possible from that of Shakespeare. Actually there were documents in Southampton's hand that showed his writing as small, neat and tidy, quite unlike the wild pot-hooks of the forgery. There was some comment on the illiteracy of the hand, but here, as in many other cases, no one bothered, apparently, to compare the forgery with the original, and it was over a year before a critic remarked their complete dissimilarity. Just before he presented the documents William realised he had made an appalling mistake; how could a letter *sent* by Shakespeare have remained in his correspondence? He solved the problem quite simply by writing above the letter, "copye of mye Letter toe hys grace offe Southampton," and submitted it to his father's joyful approval.

Shakespeare's letter was all that a poet's should be:

MYE LORDE

Doe notte esteeme me a sluggarde nor tardye for thus havynge delayed to answerre or rather toe thank you for youre greate Bountye I doe assure you my graciouse ande good Lorde that thryce I have essayed toe wryte and thryce mye efforts have benne fruitlesse I knowe notte what toe saye Prose Verse alle all is naughte gratitude is alle I have toe utter and that is tooe greate ande tooe sublyme a feeling for poore mortalls toe expresse O my Lord itte is a Budde which bllossommes bllooms butte never dyes itte cherishes sweete Nature and lulls the calme Breaste toe softe softe repose Butte mye goode Lorde forgive thys mye departure fromme mye Subjecte

which was toe retturne thankes and thankes I Doe retturne
O excuse mee mye Lorde more at presente I cannotte

> Yours devotedlye and withe due respecte
> Wm Shakspeare

And Southampton was much moved:

Deare Willam
I cannotte doe lesse than thanke you forre youre kynde
Lettere butte Whye dearest Freynd talke soe much offe
gratitude mye offerre was double the Somme butte you
woulde accepte butte the halfe thereforre you neede notte
spaeke soe muche onn thatte Subjecte as I have beene thye
Freynd soe will I continue aughte thatte I canne doe forre
thee praye commande mee ande you shalle fynde mee

> Yours
> Southampton

Julye the 4

These letters mark the true beginning of the forgeries. For the
first time William became a creator as well as a technical
imitator; the Chattertonian spelling, here first used, but later
becoming ever more intense, marks the transition from the
fabricator to the original artist. And if Samuel, his friends, and
a rapidly widening circle of the literary public had accepted the
Lease with enthusiasm, they received the letters with positive
ecstasy.

William's work was remarkably spontaneous, and most of
his forgeries seem to have been suggested by some small
coincidence or the casual word of a stranger. But behind all
their variety of subject they had a common purpose almost as
important to their author as his father's pleasure or his own
aggrandisement. Besides helping himself he wanted to help

Shakespeare, to do something to clear his idol of the slurs that had been cast upon him, and establish him as the possessor of all the personal and conventional virtues that to the eighteenth century seemed nearly as important as genius. Shakespeare was already a great poet; ideally, he must also be an eighteenth-century gentleman.

The commonest and most probable slander cast on the poet was that of Roman Catholicism. The Catholic Profession of Faith found at Stratford and alleged to be written by Shakespeare's father, coupled with certain passages in the plays, notably the Ghost's remarks on Purgatory in *Hamlet*, seemed to make a strong case for such a belief. William, "having the most rooted antipathy to everything like superstition and bigotry," determined to clear his idol of such a charge, and prove once and for all that Shakespeare was tastefully, tactfully, and undoubtedly Anglican.

Five days after producing Southampton's Letter, William handed his father Shakespeare's Profession of Faith. He had prepared the ground in his usual way by outlining the nature of his discovery before its appearance, and attempted to prove its religious importance by declaring it, as his father noted, "so sublime a piece of writing that he has learnt it through, and repeats every morning and evening in his prayer . . . he never was so perfectly convinced of the truth of the New Testament and the existence of Jesus Christ, as he has been since the discovery of this paper, and that he is fully convinced of Shakespeare being a true Christian." But in spite of this unsolicited testimonial Samuel's mind was not quite easy. He knew the manuscript was both genuine and poetic, but he could not judge its spiritual value, and so, to William's horror, he invited his learned and famous acquaintances, Dr. Parr and Dr. Warton, to call, inspect the paper, and pass their own judgment.

The two doctors were the most formidable critics William had yet encountered. Samuel Parr, the younger of the two, combined vigour, scholarship, and eccentricity into a character that brought him fame out of all proportion to his actual accomplishment. His most genuine achievements were in Education, and the rival school he established at Stanmore when the Governors declined to make him Headmaster of Harrow seems to have been one of the earliest centres of modern educational methods. Although a classical scholar, he was among the first to include English verse-composition in his curriculum, and although bell-ringing was his only exercise, he encouraged his pupils in pugilism and organised games. In spite of possessing a library of over ten thousand volumes, he published very little besides collected sermons and a Latin preface attacking Pitt with a "witty and dexterous use of the subjunctive mood." He did very little else; his immense contemporary reputation is a tribute to his remarkable personality.

Joseph Warton was a wholly different character. He, too, had been a schoolmaster, until, when Headmaster of Winchester, he was harried and driven out by the successive mutinies of pupils he was too weak to control. Unlike Parr, he was an able and prolific writer, and if his own early poetic promise had failed to flower, he achieved high repute by his critical studies of Pope and Shakespeare. Now, at seventy-three, the acknowledged patriarch of English letters, he still retained the eager enthusiasm that Dr. Johnson had delighted to parody, and was still a "voluble and ecstatic talker, often hugging his auditors in the heat of his argument." Any cause he adopted was sure of his ceaseless encouragement.

For some time the two doctors examined the appearance of the paper with the greatest care; then William was called in to describe the circumstances of his discovery. "I confess," he afterwards wrote, "I had never before felt so much terror, and would almost have bartered my life to have evaded the meeting: there was, however, no alternative, and I was under the necessity of appearing before them. Having replied to their several questionings as to the discovery of the manuscripts and the secretion of the Gentleman's name, one of these two inspectors of the manuscripts addressed me, saying, 'Well, young man; the public will have just cause to admire you for the research you have made, which will afford so much gratification to the literary world.' To this panegyric I bowed my head, and remained silent."

But the real object of the visit was to hear the content of the Profession, and they listened with close attention while Samuel read it aloud.

I beyng nowe offe sounde Mynde doe hope thatte thys mye wyshe wille atte mye deathe bee accedded toe as I nowe lyve in Londonne ande as mye soule maye perchance soone quitte thys poore Bodye it is mye desire thatte inne suche case I maybe bee carryed to mye native place ande thatte mye Bodye bee there quietlye interred wythe as little pompe as canne bee ande I doe nowe inne theese mye seyriouse Moments make thys mye professione of fayth and whiche I doe moste solemnlye believe I doe firste looke toe oune lovynge and great God ande toe hys gloriouse sonne Jesus I doe alsoe belyve thatte thys mye weake ande frayle Bodye wille retturne toe duste butte forre mye soule lette God judge

thatte as toe himselfe shalle seeme meete O omnipotente
ande greate God I am fulle offe Synne I doe notte thynke
myselfe worthye offe thye grace ande yette wille I hope forre
evene the poore prysonerre whenne bounde with gallyng
Irons evenne hee wille hope for Pittye ande whenne the
teares offe sweete repentance bathe hys wretched pillowe he
then looks ande hopes forre pardonne thenne rouze mye
Soule ande lette hope thatte sweete cherisher offe alle
afforde thee comforte alsoe O Manne whatte arte thou whye
considereste thou thyselfe thus greatlye where are thye
greate thye boasted attrybutes buryed loste forre everre inne
colde Deathe. O Manne whye attemptest thou toe searche
the greatenesse offe the Almyghtye thou doste butte loose
thye labourre more thou attempteste more arte thou loste
tille thye poore weake thoughtes arre elevated toe theyre
summite ande thence as snowe fromme the leffee Tree
droppe ande disstylle themselves tille there are noe more O
God Manne as I am frayle bye Nature fulle offe Synne yette
greate God receyve me toe thye bosomme where alle is
sweete contente ande happynesse alle is blysse where discon-
tente isse neverrre hearde butte where oune Bonde offe
freyndshippe unytes alle Menne Forgive O Lorde alle oure
synnes ande withe thye grete Goodnesse take usse alle to
thye Breaste O cherishe usse like the sweete Chickenne thatte
under the coverte offe herre spreaddynge Wings Receyves
herre lyttle Broode ande hoveringe oerre themme keepes
themme harmless ande in safetye.

WM SHAKSPEARE

There was a silence; were they going to denounce it as a
blasphemous fabrication? Then Dr. Warton said solemnly:
"Sir, we have many beautiful passages in our Litany, and in
many parts of the New Testament, but this great man has
distanced them all." William was overwhelmed by Warton's

astonishing praise. When Cowper said: "The poet who pleases a man like that has nothing left to wish for," he expressed the general opinion; the doctor's approval was the hall-mark of genius. Excusing himself from the company, William went into the back dining-room, and laid his head against the window-frame to think, while vanity and ambition consumed him like a furnace. He was not twenty years old.

Chapter Four

WILLIAM GROWS MORE AMBITIOUS

From that moment William was convinced of his own great-ness, and poured out a stream of forgeries without fear or re-straint. He wildly promised Samuel unimagined treasures from the Gent's country-house; he had seen, he said, Shakespeare's own manuscript of one of the Tragedies, while thousands of books with marginal notes in his hand filled the attics and cellars of the mysterious mansion, as well as other concrete relics that no ingenuity could counterfeit. His son had found, noted Samuel, "a seal of cornelian-stone set in gold—with the engraving of the Quintain before-mentioned—and which on examination proves to be the seal he used in sealing that Deed. This seal he is promised by the Gent shall be his. I have not yet seen it." Then there was a full-length contemporary portrait of Shake-speare in black draperies, with high, fringed gloves, one of them in his hand. The Gent had promised William this also, saying: "I am not unaware of the value of these things, and should they prove to be worth £20,000 I have given my promise that they shall be yours, and will on no consideration break my word." But in spite of this undertaking the appearance of the picture, like that of the seal, was unaccountably delayed, until Samuel began to doubt the value of the Gent's fair promises and fear that his son might be the tool of a subtle swindler.

There was, however, no withholding of literary discoveries. Early in 1795 William produced Agreements between Shake-speare, and Condell and Lowine the players, by which the latter's services were retained at a fee of a guinea a week.

These and other small legal documents of a similar nature, were primarily intended to show Shakespeare a wealthy and efficient business man, but also proved a useful support for the major forgeries, since the legal phraseology was convincingly correct and the subject-matter dull enough to be beyond suspicion. Whenever he had the time William dashed off a receipt or a note of hand, until the very size of the collection became its own validity. Imagining a forgery, however small, to be a slow and painstaking business, the majority of critics soon held it impossible for one person to have fabricated so much in less than a matter of years. It was this time-factor that proved one of the main defences of the Papers in the later controversies.

The first major attempt of the year was partly an accident. In a mood of exalted self-confidence, William made a drawing of Shakespeare's head on to old parchment, copying the likeness, to the best of his ability, from the portrait in the Folios, and ornamenting the background with grotesque faces, and shields bearing Shakespeare's arms. With the assurance of unbroken success he presented it to his father, but to his astonishment and dismay Samuel ridiculed the drawing as childish and of no consequence. Piqued at this brusque dismissal of his artistic skill, and conscious that serious doubt of one of the discoveries might reflect on the genuineness of the others, William searched the Gent's papers, and the next day discovered a letter from Shakespeare to Cowley with which the drawing had been enclosed.

WORTHYE FREYNDE

Havynge alwaye accountedde thee a Pleasaynte ande wittye Personne ande oune whose Companye I doe muche

A Whymsycalle Conceyte

esteeme I have sente thee inclosedde a whymsycalle conceyte whiche I doe suppose thou wilt easylye discoverre butte shouldst thou notte whye thenne I shalle sette thee onne mye table offe *loggerre heades*

Youre trewe Freynde
WM SHAKSPEARE.

Samuel and the Believers were delighted with such evidence of the poet's whimsical humour, and minutely examined the drawing to find the conceit it concealed. Their failure to interpret it seemed one more proof of Shakespeare's depth of mind.

The success of the drawing aroused William's interest in art, and a few days later he bought an old coloured drawing in Butcher Row. It was in water-colour on paper, one side representing a young man richly dressed in Jacobean style, and the other bearing the figure of an old bearded Dutchman with his hands in his pockets; the artist probably intending to contrast miserly father with spendthrift son. It occurred to William that the Dutchman bore some faint resemblance to Shylock, and to make the likeness still clearer he painted in the background a knife and a pair of scales. Behind the figure of the young man he drew Shakespeare's initials, arms (wrongly drawn and coloured), and the titles of some of the plays; altered the face as much as he dared so as to resemble the Folio portrait, and presented the result to his father. As usual, Samuel and his friends believed immediately, and then sought for justification. It was decided that the young man represented Bassanio in the *Merchant of Venice*, with Shakespeare himself taking the part, and it was surmised that the drawing had formerly hung in the Green Room of the Globe Theatre. Mr. Hewlett of the

Common Pleas office, an acknowledged expert on old hand-writing, examined the discovery, and detected in the background a signature of John Hoskins, a seventeenth-century painter. In Samuel's facsimile the name stands out clearly; in the original painting it could only be seen by such experts as the one who discovered it.

Shakespeare was now established as wit, business man, and friend of the great; the next step was to show his simple humanity. For some days William searched the Gent's papers with provoking unsuccess; then announced a discovery more exciting than any of its predecessors: a love letter to Ann Hathaway written by the poet during his courtship, and, enclosed with it, a lock of his own hair. The enclosure of the hair, and possibly the writing of the whole letter, had been suggested to William by the chance purchase of some royal patents of Henry VIII and Elizabeth. In such documents the Great Seal was pendent not from the usual parchment strip, but on a piece of thick woven silk of a quality and distinguished appearance that demanded use in the forgeries. A lock of hair William had been given as a love token made a really impressive relic when tied with this royal silk; it was convincing enough to support even the accompanying letter.

The youthful Shakespeare was at once ardent and poetic:

DEARESSTE ANNA

As thou haste alwaye founde mee toe mye Worde moste trewe soe shalt thou see I have stryctlye kepte mye promyse I praye you perfume thys mye poore Locke withe thye balmye Kysses forre thenne indeede shalle Kynges themmeselves bowe ande paye homage toe itte I do assure thee no rude hande hathe knottedde itte thye Willys alone hath

done the worke Neytherre the gyldedde bawble thatte envyronnes the heade of Majestye noe norre honourres moste
weyghtye wulde give mee halfe the joye as didde thysse mye
lyttle worke forre thee The feelinge thatte dydde neareste
approache untoe itte was thatte whiche commethe nygheste
untoe God meeke ande Gentle Charytye forre thatte Virrtue
O Anna doe I love doe I cheryshe thee inne mye hearte forre
thou arte ass a talle Cedarre stretchynge forthe its branches
ande succourynge smaller Plants fromme nyppynge Winne-
terre orr the boysterouse Wyndes Farewelle toe Morrowe bye
tymes I wille see thee tille thenne Adewe sweete Love

Thyne everre
Wм Shakspeare

Anna Hatherrewaye

Enclosed with this letter was a poem:

> *Is there inne heavenne aught more rare*
> *Thanne thou sweete Nymphe of Avon fayre*
> *Is there onne Earthe a Manne more trewe*
> *Thanne Willy Shakspeare is toe you*
>
> *Though fyckle fortune prove unkynde*
> *Stille dothe she leave herre wealthe behynde*
> *She neere the hearte canne forme anew*
> *Norre make thye Willys love unnetrue*
>
> *Though Age withe witherd hand doe stryke*
> *The forme moste fayre the face moste bryghte*
> *Still dothe she leave unnetouchedde ande trewe*
> *Thy Willys love ande freynshyppe too*
>
> *Though deathe with neverre faylynge blowe*
> *Dothe Manne ande babe alyke brynge lowe*
> *Yette doth he take naughte butte hys due*
> *Ande strikes notte Willys hearte stille trewe*

Synce thenne norre forretune deathe norre Age
Canne faythfulle Willys love asswage
Thenne doe I live and dye forre you
Thy Willy syncere and moste trewe

The admirers of the manuscripts were delighted with such youthful enthusiasm, agreeing with James Boaden, editor of the *Oracle*, that the letter was "distinguished by the utmost delicacy of passion and poetical spirit," while others, not content with such prosaic adoration, reverently extracted hairs from the divine lock and wore them on their fingers set in gold rings. Samuel himself was especially pleased to find reminiscences of the letter in Shakespeare's later work, and quoted with approval from *Henry VI*, Part III:

> "*Thus yields the Cedar to the Axes edge*
> *Whose arms gave shelter to the princely Eagle,*
> *Under whose shade the ramping Lyon slept,*
> *Whose top branch over-peered Joves spreading Tree,*
> *And kept low shrubs from Winter's powerful wind.*"

Beautiful lines! It was pleasant to think that Anna had been their inspiration.

There was still another service to be done for Shakespeare. William had often heard his father's friend, the Hon. John Byng, speak of a letter supposed to have been written to the poet by James I which, had it still existed, would have been final proof of the social standing of its recipient. Even William dared not take so obvious a hint, but a fortnight later, towards the end of February, he copied Queen Elizabeth's signature from a facsimile in his father's library, and produced the most charming of notes from the Queen to the poet.

Elizabeth was more than friendly, she was almost chatty:

Wee didde receive youre prettye Verses goode Masterre William through the hands off oure Lorde Chamberlayne ande wee doe Complemente thee onne theyre great excellenceWee shalle departe fromme Londonne toe Hamptowne forre the holydayes where wee Shalle expecte thee withe thye beste Actorres thatte thou mayste playe before oureselfe toe amuse usse bee notte slowe butte comme toe usse bye Tuesdaye nexte asse the lorde Leiscesterre wille bee withe usse

ELIZABETH R.

Thys Letterre I dydde receyve fromme mye moste gracyouse Ladye Elyzabethe ande I doe requeste itte maye bee kepte withe alle care possyble

WM SHAKSPEARE

For Master William Shakspeare atte the Globe bye Thames.

What doubt could there be now of the poet's gentility? "We think it clearly proves," wrote Boaden in the *Oracle*, "that all this degrading nonsense of him holding horses, etc., will be found utterly fictitious, and that this great man was the Garrick of his age, caressed by everyone great and illustrious. . . ."

As early as December, 1794, William had told his father that a complete manuscript of one of the tragedies lay in the Gent's country house, but he had not produced or even named his discovery, for fear of the work involved, and because he lacked a sufficiently early text to take as model. At the beginning of the year, when Samuel began to press for more details, he fortunately acquired the quarto edition of *Lear*, which William immediately began to copy out in the old hand. He made occasional major, and innumerable minor textual alterations, all with the common purpose of purging the crudity, roughness, and down-right vulgarity that marred many of Shakespeare's most elevated passages. In doing so Ireland was only following the practice of his age. It was a commonplace of eighteenth-century criticism that Shakespeare, or at least his text, was regrettably crude and unpolished; in William's own words "it was gener-ally deemed very extraordinary that the productions of Shakespeare should be found so very unequal, and in particular that so much ribaldry should appear throughout his dramatic compositions." He determined to knock the coarseness out of *Lear*, and bring it to a refined perfection that would have pleased Pope and satisfied Johnson; in the opinion of most of his readers he succeeded. "It presents a style," wrote Samuel, comparing the new manuscript with the printed versions of the play, "as undressed as it is uniform; and so much so, that the Editor is thoroughly assured that whoever will give himself the trouble of collating a few scenes, must, if he has the smallest critical sagacity, be able to pronounce for himself with certainty as to almost every instance, in which the general style of the author is departed from and a new one substituted; and that instead of his simple phraseology and sentences, framed according to their natural order and construction, the obvious general features of his own writings, there will be found at intervals tumor and gaudy trappings, and hardness, and inversion."

Samuel, in fact, thoroughly approved of the alterations.

Shakespeare introduced his manuscript in modest fashion. "If fromme Masterre Hollinneshedde," he apologises on the first page, "I have inne somme lyttle departetedde fromme hymme butte thatte Libbertye will notte I truste be blamedde

44

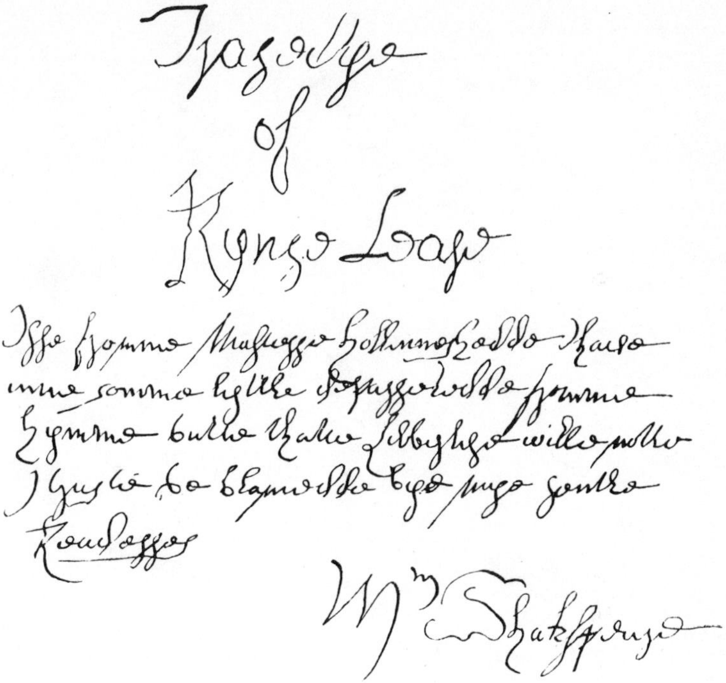

Tragedye
of
Kynge Leare

Isse Fromme Masterre Hollinneshedde Ihave
inne somme lyttle departedde fromme
hymme butte thatte Libbertye wille notte
I truste be blamedde bye mye gentle
Readerres

Wm Shakspeare

The Manuscript of "Lear"

bye mye gentle Readerres." He proved to have departed as much from his printed text as from his sources.

The eighteenth century was impatient of subtlety, and the obscurities that now delight the Shakespearian scholar were then regarded as distasteful blots on the lucid clarity that best became a poet. William, of course, shared these standards, and his alterations from the quarto text were as much to clarify meaning as to purge vulgarity. If his vocabulary and powers of interpretation were even lower than those of his contemporaries, and sometimes led him to amend for the worse the already obvious, so much the more credit to Shakespeare's painstaking simplicity. In his preface to the publication of the new manuscript, Samuel quoted a few of the emendations that particularly pleased him.

Where the quarto has:

> *Tripped me behind, being down, insulted railed*
> *And put upon him such a deal of man*
> *That worthied him, got praises of the king,*
> *For him attempting who was self subdued*
> *And in the flechuent of this dread exploit*
> *Drew on me here again . . .*

the manuscript substituted:

> *Tripped mee behynde beyinge downe, insultedde, raylde*
> *Ande putte onne hymme soe muche o the Manne*
> *Thatte worthyedde hymme ande gotte hymme prayses o the Kynge*
> *Ande forre the Attempt of thys hys softe subdud exployte*
> *Drewe oune mee here agayne. . . .*

Presumably William found "flechuent" too much for him, but it is difficult to see why he imagined that Shakespeare would have preferred the Alexandrine to his ordinary metre, and still

more curious that Shakespearian fanatics such as Samuel and his
friends should have allowed anything but the strictest of blank
verse. Perhaps the faint echo of the Augustans brought a
drifting rumour of added refinement.

Again, the hastening thought of:

> I would divorce me from thy mother's tomb
> Sepulchring an adultress . . .

becomes in the new canon:

> I would divorce thee fromme thye Motherres Wombe
> Ande saye the Motherre was an Adultresse . . .

which was widely considered to be much the more sensible
reading.

William himself took most pride in his purely poetical
improvements on the printed text. Wherever opportunity
offered he replaced common epithets by others more beautiful,
and occasionally inserted whole passages of his own composition. In the printed play Kent bids farewell to the world after
Lear's death, with:

> I have a journey, sir, shortly to go
> My master calls and I must not say no,

which William rightly considered jingling and pedestrian in
the extreme, and poeticised to:

> Thanks, sir, butte I goe toe thatte unknowne Land
> Thatte Chaynes each Pilgrim faste within its Soyle
> Bye livynge menne mouste shunned mouste dreadedde
> Stille mye goode masterre thys same Journey tooke
> He calls mee I amme contente ande strayght obeye
> Thenne farewelle Worlde the busye Sceane is done
> Kente livd mouste true Kente dyes mouste lyke a Manne.

Both Samuel and their author held the lines to be no little improvement.

In the long and arduous work of copying out the whole play into the old handwriting, William, either through carelessness, or to lighten an exceedingly dull task, permitted himself the most extravagant spellings, and utterly outdid the worst excesses of Chatterton. *Dymennesyonnes, innetennecyonne,* or *attennedauntes* were bad enough, *Gennetellemanne* and *Perrepennedycularely*[1] superbly worse, but *glosterre exitte* was absolutely impossible. Curiously enough, such orthography made very little impression; the opponents jeered at, and the supporters justified it, but for a long time no one stressed its full enormity. Unfortunately, there was no attempt to explain it on the ground of Shakespeare's poor education.

Lear was a great success, and William intended to follow it up by discovering a similar manuscript of *Hamblette.* But the work was too laborious for his active ambition, and he abandoned it after a few pages of the usual omissions and alterations.[2]

Of all the forgeries, the altered *Lear* was easily the most

[1] Dimensions, intention, attendants, gentleman, perpendicularly.

[2] The few leaves of *Hamblette* he did produce were mostly from the play scene and the scenes with Ophelia. Typical of his refining influence on the original is the omission of:

Ham.: That's a fair thought to lie between a maid's legs.
Oph.: What is, my lord?
Ham.: Nothing.

But most of the changes were such emendations as the replacement of:
"What means your Lordship?"
by
"Mye Godde Lorde whatte meanes youre honoure."
Ireland seems to have loved redundancy.

successful. "A better Shakespeare rises to our view," cries one enthusiast, "which we evidently see in this his own written play of *Lear*—by comparing which with the printed copies, we shall perceive how it has lost in them its purity, energy, and spirit; how it has been deformed by the bold hand of a meddling printer or his devil." Most of the readers wholly agreed with him.

But the experts were not yet done with *Lear*. Francis Webb, secretary at the College of Heralds, remarked a few scrawled signs and figures on the last page of the manuscript. William had made them casually, or even unconsciously, in the idle relaxation of completing the work, but to Mr. Webb they looked very like shorthand, a subject on which he fancied his expert knowledge, and he borrowed the page to give them a closer study. Even an expert, unfortunately, could not twist the markings into sense, but Webb made the best of a bad job with the ingenuous fervour to be expected of a former Nonconformist preacher. "I think the whole that can be concluded from this fragment," he reported to Samuel, "is, that this great Man was ever employed, and did attempt shorthand. But if among other precious and valuable relics of this immortal Man no more attempts are found, I should conclude that his great and active Mind found the attempt too minute, tedious and [onerous], and therefore desisted. On the whole, I think it happy for the world that he made no further Advances; as it might have prevented his writing so legibly and at length as he has done, especially in these precious relics now before me." Can we wonder that the forgeries won so easy a success?

For some months William let well alone and made no more

discoveries. In any case, he was too busy to have much opportunity, for his new-found popularity with his father's friends, and the delightful duty of showing the Papers to visitors, took away both leisure and inclination for the solitary hard work that further fabrication would require. But in June the urge to repeat his triumphs became too strong, and he brought home the most reckless of all his surprising discoveries; a Deed of Gift from William Shakespeare to his friend Masterre William Henrye Irelande.

I William Shakspeare . . . doe make ande ordeyne thys as ande for mye deede of Gyfte for inn as muche as life is mouste precyouse toe alle menne soe shoulde bee thatte personne who att the peryle of hys owne shalle save thatte of a fellowe Createure Bearying thys inn Mynde ande havyng beene soe savedde myeselfe I didd withe myne owne hande fyrste wryte on Papere the conntennts hereof butte for the moure securytye ande thatte noe dyspute whatever myghte happenne afterre mye deathe I have nowe causedd the same toe bee written onn Parchemente and have heretoe duly sett and affyxedd mye hande and Seale Whereas onne or abowte the thyrde day of laste monethe beyng the monethe of Auguste havynge withe mye goode freynde Masterre William Henrye Irelande ande otherres taene boate neare untowe myne house afowresayde wee dydde purpose goynge upp Thames butte those thatte were soe toe connducte us beynge muche toe merrye throughe Lyquorre theye didde upsette oure fowresayde bayrge alle butte mye selfe savedd themselves by swimmynge for though the Waterre was deepe yette owre beynge close nygh toe shore made itte lyttel dyffyculte for themm knowinge the fowresayde Art Masterre William henrye Irelande nott seeynge mee dydd aske for mee butte oune of the Companye dydd answeree thatte I was drownyinge onn the whyche he pulledd off hys Jerrekynne ande Jumpedd inn afterre me withe muche paynes he draggedd mee forthe I beynge then nearelye deade ande soe he dydd save mye life and for the whyche Service I doe herebye give hym as folowithe!!! Fyrste mye writtenn Playe of Henrye fowrthe Henrye fyfthe Kyng John Kyng Leare as allsoe mye written Playe neverr yett imprintedd whych I have named Kyng henrye thyrde of Englande alle the profyttes of the whych are whollye toe be for sayde Ireland ande atte hys deathe thenne to hys fyrste Sonne namedd alsoe William henrye . . . ande soe on for everre in hys lyne. . . .

With this solemn Deed Shakespeare enclosed lines of a more personal and sprightly nature:

Givenne toe mye mouste worthye
ande excellaunte Freynde Masterre
William Henrye Irelande inne
Remembraunce of hys havynge
Savedde mye life whenne onne
Thames
WILLIAM SHAKSPEARE

Inne life wee
wille live togetherre
Deathe
shalle forre a lytelle
parte usse butte
Shakespeares Soule restelesse
inne the Grave shalle uppe
Agayne ande meete hys freynde hys
IRELAND
Inne the Bleste Courte of Heavenne

O Modelle of Virretue Charytyes Sweeteste
Chylde thye Shakspeare thanks thee

50

Norre Verse norre Sygh norre Teare canne
Paynte mye Soule norre saye bye
halfe howe muche I love thee
                    Thyne
                           Wm. SHAKSPEARE

Keepe thys forre mee ande shoude the Worlde
prove sowerre rememberre oune lives thatte
loves the stylle.

On either side of this moving promise were drawn the Arms
of Ireland and his friend joined by a chain.[1] Even in moments
of deep emotion Shakespeare could not entirely repress his
lovable humour, and along with these affecting declarations
he sent a sketch of the Jacobean Ireland's large and splendid,
if architecturally curious, house, with the endearing subscrip-
tion:

Viewe o mye Masterre Irelands house bye the whyche
I doe showe thatte hee hath falselye sayde inne tellynge mee
I knewe notte howe toe showe itte hymme onne Paperre ande
bye the whyche I ha wonne fromme (him) the Summe o
5 shyllynges
                           W. SHAKSPEARE

Technically, these papers are among the best of the forgeries. The handwriting is natural and assured, and the
spelling consistent, while the documents were convincingly
enclosed in a stiff parchment cover with leather strings. Even
the contents were not so outrageous as might at first appear.
Shakespeare had in fact had dealings with an Ireland, although
there is no evidence of other than a business relationship; for a

[1] Sir Isaac Heard, Garter King-at-Arms, suggested that this gave Samuel
sufficient ground for coupling his arms with those of Shakespeare.

person of that name had occupied the Blackfriars property which the poet bought in 1612. This, or some earlier Ireland, was a man of sufficient substance to be remembered in his neighbourhood, for in Samuel's time the yard where the property had stood was still known as *Ireland's Yard*. Had the Deed been discovered by itself, and brought forward by someone bearing a different name, it might well have gained some credence. As it was, it awoke suspicions even among the staunchest of the believers.

Apart from William's increasing paranoia and his natural desire to get some personal credit from his work, there was a very good reason for making such a discovery. As the bulk and importance of the Papers increased, they offered prospects of considerable profit, and some even among Samuel's friends began to question his right, which he sometimes stressed rather tactlessly, to have complete control of the treasures. If, it was said, the Gent. had abandoned all claim to the property, it should go to the Nation, or at least to some independent body, and even if the owner had not entirely renounced his rights, it was surely best that such precious remains should be in the keeping of a committee rather than of a single individual. The Deed of Gift was the only possible answer.

These latest discoveries were, for a time, accepted without special question. There was nothing for a believer to bring against them save an illogical sense of proportion he had long since abandoned, while the opposition gained more ammunition for public controversy and support for their own private convictions, than definite evidence to urge against the Papers as a whole. The hostile *Morning Herald* observed that:

The *swimming* reasons given in a paper of yesterday in favor of the authenticity of certain *musty manuscripts*, shew to what Dangers we may expose ourselves by *wading* too far in pursuit of an *object*.

which probably expressed the feelings of all who still kept their critical senses.

Besides the major forgeries, William, in the belief that the greater the bulk the stronger the conviction, produced a large number of notes, scraps, and receipts relating to Shakespeare's theatrical business. One of the most interesting of these fragments, a receipt for expenses incurred for playing "before the Lorde Leycesterre," has the dated corner missing, and William tells us that he nearly betrayed himself by dating it two years after his lordship's death, but fortunately found his mistake in time and tore off the corner before he presented it for inspection. Edmund Malone directly accuses Samuel of himself detecting the mistake and removing the date, and it certainly seems strange that William, who always precipitately presented his forgeries when the ink was hardly dry, should have chanced to discover his mistake in the short time between completion and presentation. Perhaps Samuel *did* find a mistake, and realised that Shakespeare's clerical error would upset the whole splendid edifice of his rediscovered genius. The Papers were genuine; should a casual slip in the menial task of a business man be allowed to destroy the repute of the greatest poet in history? Conscience would not only permit, it would almost command Samuel gently to pull at the corner of the Receipt until the tattered parchment came away.

From the beginning of the year William had been engaged

on the easier but equally impressive task of producing Shakespeare's library. He had told his father of stacks of old books, many of them signed and annotated in the poet's own hand, that lay in the Gent's country house, and throughout the spring hardly a week passed without the discovery of volumes that finally disproved the slanders on their owner's education. William was something of an expert on old books, and we may surmise that after his wonderful discovery Samuel allowed him more money. At any rate, whether by fortune or knowledge, he succeeded in acquiring a great number of sixteenth and seventeenth-century works, many of them of extreme rarity, and his father was delighted to find at least one book of which he had never heard, and others of which only single copies were known to exist.

Shakespeare's library was found to include the widest variety of subjects, and his marginal comments showed an humane and cultivated mind. On his copy of a pamphlet relating to Guy Fawkes, the poet noted that he had been asked to attend the traitor's execution, but that he "lykedde notte toe beholde syghtes of thatte kynde." Unfortunately for his effort to show the writer's philanthropic disposition, William had added that he had conversed with "misterre Guy Fawkes" at the Globe Theatre, forgetting that "Fawkes" was a name assumed only for the conspiracy. But, as usual, nobody noticed the error till many months afterwards. Shakespeare deplored vulgarity even in the work of others, and his copy of Bartholomeus' *De Proprietatibus Rerum* has the antique crudity of "ballocke-stones" carefully erased, and replaced by "stones of generation." William was especially anxious to prove his idol's learning, and generally showed his understanding of foreign languages by copiously marking passages where they occurred. His own ignorance prevented verbal annotation, but even his markings sometimes betrayed him, and he abruptly ends the underlining of a Latin quotation in the middle of the vital sentence. But, even apart from their notes and comments, the books themselves were a valuable and impressive collection, and did much, at a later stage, to support the authenticity of the Papers.

Very soon after the first of the forgeries William's fevered ambition drove him to the greatest of all his resolutions, and he promised his father a complete and hitherto unknown tragedy that surpassed all those that preceded it. Samuel, as always, his son's unwitting Mephistopheles, suggested the plot by one of his own engravings, depicting Rowena offering wine to Vortigern, that hung above the mantelpiece of his study. William's attention was suddenly caught by this familiar object, he referred to Holinshed, found the story suitable, and, before a line was written, described in flamboyant detail the manuscript of Shakespeare's *King Vortigern*.

Samuel, stirred to the depths of his easy enthusiasm, continually pressed his son to bring home this new wonder, and William was forced to produce a few pages at a time written in his own hand, with the explanation that the Gent. forbade the removal of the play until he had made a complete copy. All through the spring the manuscript came in, page by page, and William transcribed it on to parchment as fast as his leisure permitted. Reports of this greatest discovery caught the public imagination, and stirred the curious eddy round Norfolk Street into a whirlpool. But Samuel showed *King Vortigern* to no one.

Chapter Five

PUBLIC OPINION

From the beginning, the Papers attracted a great deal of attention. Samuel's guileless delight in his new wonder welcomed every visitor, and he eagerly displayed the precious relics to anyone who could claim the slightest of common acquaintance. Not for a moment had he doubted that every candid and ingenious observer would immediately accept the authenticity of the manuscripts, and it came as a great shock to find that spiteful and malevolent persons, veiling their envious enmity under the specious guise of criticism, were prepared to remain hostile to the discoveries even after a personal inspection. Samuel's earliest belief and oft-quoted platitude was that "truth will find its basis," but he soon realised that, for the present at any rate, the Papers must be guarded from those who did not see the distinction between criticism and sacrilege.

The first, most persistent and most dangerous of the doubters was Edmund Malone. Tiring at an early age of the Irish Bar, Malone had come to England and devoted his enormous energies to literary criticism. By middle age he was famous and respected; as popular with the great for his wit and hospitality as he was feared by the scholar for his devastating research and relentless campaign against the slipshod and inaccurate. He never lost the ferocity and mocking invective of a Dublin barrister, and hounded the errors of long-dead Shakespearian editors with as much enthusiasm as he demolished his living competitors.

By the time of the Forgeries he had quite eclipsed George

Steevens, Johnson's editorial collaborator and his own former patron, and was generally regarded as the leading authority on Shakespeare, whom he purified and edited with a painstaking scholarship that was only marred by his unshakable obstinacy. At his worst he was an intellectual vandal, and it is typical of this side of his character that he compelled the vicar of Stratford to whitewash the coloured bust of Shakespeare which stood in the chancel of the church. One of his many enemies celebrated this occasion in bitter verse:

> *Stranger, to whom this monument is known*
> *Invoke the Poet's curse upon Malone*
> *Whose meddling zeal his barbarous taste displays*
> *And daubs his tombstone as he marrs his plays.*

But it took more than a taunt to deter Malone.

Such a man was the complete antithesis of Samuel Ireland, and any contact between them was bound to have ended in enmity. Malone's laborious and rudely expressed critiques annoyed Samuel as much as his own muddled antiquarianism must have exasperated the critic, and even had Malone felt inclined to credit the possibility of the discoveries, he would probably have opposed them in disgust at the general adulation. As it was, he doubted their authenticity from the very first, and scented with delight a controversy beside which the Chatterton affair would appear the merest ripple.

Malone was extremely anxious to avoid making a formal inspection of the manuscripts, as he knew by long experience that were he unable to disprove the Papers at his first examination, it would be given out that he had accepted them, and any subsequent criticism would be put down to envy or corruption.

He endeavoured, therefore, to see the discoveries on neutral territory, and sent Humphrey the engraver to leave his card on Mr. Caldecott, with whom both he and Samuel were acquainted, requesting that he might call on him and inspect the manuscripts at his chambers. Here he made a serious mistake. Caldecott fancied himself a Shakespearian scholar, and spent much of his time collecting Shakespeariana and preparing an extremely feeble edition of *Hamlet*. He hated Malone for a bad critic and successful rival, and it must have given him the greatest pleasure to inform this unexpected suppliant that the Papers "would not be removed for any person whatever, unless Mr. I. should be requested to wait on His Majesty with them, which he should certainly, as his duty required, comply with. At the same time Mr. Caldecott informed Mr. Humphrey that he believed it was Mr. Ireland's intention not to show them to any Commentator or Shakespeare-monger whatever."

But Malone was not so easily snubbed, and "in a very unbecoming and ungentlemanlike manner," made another outrageous request. "If you can get your friend to bring Lord Southampton's letter, and the answer to it, and the articles between Condelle and Hemynge etc., to your house to-morrow at three o'clock," he wrote to the Hon. John Byng, "I will produce a facsimile of Lord Southampton's handwriting which will at once ascertain the matter, but I beg my name may not be mentioned, let it be only a *gentleman*." Samuel gave his opinion that a *gentleman* would be a most unsuitable disguise for Mr. Malone, and refused to consider any but a public visit. From that time Malone and the Irelands were open enemies.

Shortly afterwards, Samuel found another dangerous opponent in Henry Bate Dudley, editor of the *Morning Herald* and one of the ablest black sheep of his period. From his days as a young curate, when he neglected his flock to go duelling and debauching nightly in Vauxhall Gardens, to his magistracy in Ireland and surprising acquirement of a baronetcy, Dudley led a turbulent and exciting life in which expulsions and prosecutions for simony went side by side with enormous popularity as a Grub Street journalist. At the time of the Forgeries his editorship gave him considerable influence, and Samuel had hopes that his friendship with Pearce, Dudley's brother-in-law, might be of great help in spreading the fame of the Shakespeare treasures.

This attempt to pull strings proved singularly unfortunate, and whether in spite or because of Pearce's efforts, Dudley's first mention of the manuscripts was insulting in the extreme:

SHAKESPEARE

The SHAKESPEARE *discoveries*, said to have been made by the son of Mr. IRELAND of Norfolk Street, are the Tragedy of LEAR, and another entitled VORTIGERN, now first brought to light, both in the Bard's own handwriting. In the same chest are said to have been also found an antique MELANGE of *love-letters! professions of faith! billets-doux! locks of hair! and family receipts!*—The only danger as to *faith in the discovery* seems to be from the indiscretion of *protesting too much*.

Samuel was amazed and furious at this slander, and immediately sought out Pearce, urging him to show his brother-in-law the enormity of his conduct. But Pearce weakly protested that he had no influence with, indeed had long been estranged from, his difficult relation, and suggested that Samuel himself should call on Dudley at the offices of the *Morning Herald*. For some days Mr. Ireland might have been seen stamping up and down

Fleet Street, waiting in vain for Mr. Dudley to arrive or return, and hearing, with as much good temper as he could feign, that the gentleman he saw entering just then could not possibly have been the editor, and that unfortunately no one in the office knew who was the author of the *Herald's* numerous offensive paragraphs. At last, his patience exhausted, Samuel wrote his elusive quarry a strong letter:

> . . . The paragraph to which I allude is under the article *Shakespeare*. It contains insinuations of so malevolent and injurious a Nature reflecting the reputation of myself and family as to render it necessary to know from you, whether it meets the public eye with your concurrence or not. If it has not passed your immediate observation I then request that it may in to-morrow's Herald be so stated as to contain truths only, which as it now stands it is *totally destitute* of. . . .

But Dudley merely replied:

> Your letter to me is of so extraordinary a kind, that you must allow me to decline giving you any further answer than acknowledging the receipt of it.

The Papers had made another enemy.

Unlike Malone, Dudley was not malicious, and the *Morning Herald*, though hostile to the Papers, contented itself mainly with harmless parodies that were neither intended nor taken very seriously. The most famous of these was *The Great Literary Trial of Vortigern and Rowena*. The Trial, which took place under the presidency of Polonius, was an attack less on the Papers than on the contemporary celebrities who formed the jury. Every social and political figure whom Dudley wished to flatter or offend, was supposed to express an opinion on the genuineness of the play, by quoting an appropriate passage from it. The "quotations," of course, had personal references to their supposed sponsors, and were clever specimens of the usual Grub Street satire. Thus George Steevens, the Shakespearian editor, was made to select:

He was by 'an indenture to wit' apprenticed to a twister of common-sense, and afterwards set up fancie-monger on his own botomme; he lives now by stitching motley buttons on dead *Bards'* jackets! And yet this varlet has humour; for he'll laugh you till his sides crack, at his own comical disfigurements!

while Lady A—— was supposed to choose:

> . . . *Mine was the earlie arte*
> *To banish Nature's blushes from the cheeke.*
> *I learnt it of a Dyer's wife in SPAINE*
> *Whose face in Tyrian dye was so engrained*
> *That* turkie cockes *assailed her as she passed.*

The *Trial,* which had been intended as a passing joke, became so popular that it was continued for months and finally published in a book that went through several editions. Dudley kept up the pretence of quotation with such effect that many people believed the passages to be genuine extracts from the much-discussed *Vortigern,* and Samuel had to publish an official denial in the *Oracle*:

Mr. IRELAND feels it a duty he owes to the fame of our GREAT BARD, to the PUBLIC, and to HIMSELF, to declare, that not a single line has been permitted to be copied, nor shall it be, till it is published. . . .

Dudley was so pleased with the success of his imitations that

61

he forgot malice, and for a time ceased his campaign against the Shakespeare Papers.

Other newspapers also tried their hand at parody, and published excerpts from remarkable documents said to have been found in their attics. The *Telegraph* recovered such valuable material on Shakespeare's domestic life as:

Too Misstere Joonnesse, Cheessemongerree.
SIRREE
Thee cheesesse youe sentte mee werre tooe sweattie, ande tooe rankee in flavourre, butte thee redde herringges weere addmirabblee. Mye dearre friendde Johnn O'Coombee is parrticcullarriee fonde of neatesse tonngueesse soe praie sendde mee a dozzene offe them andde a ferrkenne off freshee buttere fore mie loovelie misse Annee Haathawaye.

and:

Tooo Missteerree Beenjaammiinnee Joohnnssonn
DEEREE SIRREE,
Wille youe doee meee theee favvourree too dinnee wythee meee onnn Friddaye nextte attt twoo off theee clockee too eatee sommee muttonne choppes andd somme poottaattooeesse
I amm deerree sirree
Yourre goodde friendde
WILLIAME SHAEKSPARE.

Another paper discovered manuscripts of greater historical importance, and published a letter from Queen Elizabeth to the poet:

We give thee nottice thatte wee shalle drinke tea withe thee bye Thames to-morrowe, thou monarche offe the *Globe*. Inne thy Hamblette wee perceive thou didst oure biddinge twittinge mye Lorde of Leicesterre thatte he was fatte and

"The Gold Mines of Ireland"

From a contemporary print in the British Museum

scante of breathe. Write mee whatte thou thinkeste offe the lankye Ladde Southamptowne thye friende. . . .

P.S. More offe oure virgin beautie.

But most of the Press was at first wholly favourable, and printed nothing at which even Samuel could easily take offence.

More important than the anonymous opinions of the newspapers were the personal views of the ordinary literary public. His unfortunate experiences with Dudley and Malone had warned Samuel against the dangers of premature publicity, and he resolved to exhibit the Papers no further until he had sufficient evidence definitely to prove their authenticity. "My son and I," he wrote early in February of 1795, "have determined on shutting out all Shakespeare-mongers—(? in) course the great heroes in that line have ample doubts—particularly with regard to whole plays being found—*that*, they boldly say, cannot be true. This illiberal disbelief of my assertions, which has been thrown out by others as well as the Commentators, has induced me to determine to show the papers no further at present, till by showing the Lear we can give them a flat contradiction. . . ." Very great store was set by the manuscript of *Lear*, and many who frankly admitted their incompetence to pass judgment on handwriting, parchment, or notes of hand, felt that here was a test that could admit of no deception. If the written manuscript was superior to the printed play, then Shakespeare and none other must be its author.

Lear, as we have seen, was an unqualified success. "In the title-page," wrote the *Oracle*, approvingly, "the great Bard professes to have taken the story from HOLINSHEAD; and has, in the true spirit of modesty, apologised for the liberty he took in departing from the exact statement of the chronicle. Our suspicions of the *licentious* passages are confirmed by this the original!—they are not SHAKESPEARE'S, but the foisted impurities of buffoons upon the Theatre, recorded in the prompt books.''

The refinement and superiority of the new manuscripts gave the most satisfying explanation for the hostility of the great Commentators. "If this be the case with this play," wrote Mr. Webb, the shorthand expert, "have we not reason to suppose that other plays, if not all of Shakespeare's which are come down to us, have been thus altered, mutilated, and debased? A humiliating thought, especially to his learned Commentators, who must be mortified, when they reflect how much Die, Sweat, and Ink they have expended in explaining the obscure and rectifying the erroneous passages in the Writings of our immortal Bard; which, after all their labour, they will perhaps now be forced to acknowledge, were never his, but chargeable alone to the impertinent folly, blundering Ignorance, or arragant conceit of a Printer or Actor. Hinc illæ lachrymæ of the confederate cohort of modern Commentators; who, before they have seen or examined, presume to pass judgment, impeaching the manifest and indubitable Authenticity of these invaluable additions to the Works of our venerable Bard." And, if you really believed the emendations were improvements, there was nothing more to say.

The enthusiastic reception of *Lear* determined Samuel to publish the manuscripts in book form, and subscriptions were invited for the *Miscellaneous Papers* . . . . *of William Shakespeare*, with coloured facsimiles and a critical introduction, to be published at the end of the year in a handsome folio volume, uniform

with the definitive edition of the Works then printing at the
Shakespeare Press. The price was the considerable one of four
guineas, but over a hundred and twenty people are listed as
subscribers, including Boswell, Sotheby, Sheridan, the Duke
of Leeds, Viscount Torrington and Mr. and Mrs. Warren
Hastings. An additional inducement to subscribers was the
allotment of tickets to inspect the Papers at Samuel's house in
Norfolk Street, on Mondays, Wednesdays and Fridays between
12 and 3. This public exhibition soon became one of the
sights of the town; printed tickets were issued, and Samuel,
William, or Miss Ireland showed the visitors round,
and, we may presume, delivered an explanatory lecture.
Samuel afterwards claimed to have lost money over the
publication, but as practically every wealthy collector and
antiquarian in the city must have visited the relics, and as
many of them probably stayed to examine their host's books
and pictures, we may guess that Samuel did well enough out
of his son's discovery.

The Exhibition brought a stream of testimonials. "All great
and eminent Geniuses," wrote the inevitable Webb, "have
their characteristic peculiarities and originality of character,
which not only *distinguish* them from *all others,* but *make* them
what they are. There none can rival, none successfully imitate.
Of all men and Poets, perhaps Shakespeare had the most of
these. He was a peculiar Being—a unique—he stood alone. To
imitate him, so as to pass the deceit upon the world, were
impossible . . . [the Papers] bear indubitable proofs of his
sublime genius, boundless imagination, pregnant wit, and
intuitive sagacity into the workings of the human mind, and
evolution of the passions. . . . It must be Shakespeare's and

Shakespeare's only. It either comes from his pen or from Heaven."[1]

"His Heavenly prayer to Christ as God-Man," chimed Dr. Spence, "and his beautiful Allusion to the chickenne deserve to go through many Editions together . . . the reading of it made me say from my heart, Amen. At the same time many find fault with the word chickenne."

But others would have none of this fault-finding. "They are (without a figure) written by the unerring hand of Nature in the character of Heaven, and we read them by the steady light of Truth. They are like the stars of the firmament for number, and clear as the meridian sun. I mean this as a calm description." What were the sneers of the *Morning Herald* beside such tributes as these?

On February 20th, James Boswell came to Norfolk Street. For some time he closely examined the Papers with a running comment of joy and admiration. "At length, finding himself rather thirsty, he requested a tumbler of warm brandy and water; which having nearly finished, he then redoubled his praise of the manuscripts; and at length, rising from his chair, he made use of the following expression: 'Well; I shall now die contented, since I have lived to witness the present day.' Mr. Boswell then, kneeling down before the volume containing a portion of the Papers, continued: 'I now kiss the invaluable relics of our Bard: and thanks to God that I have lived to see them!' "[2]

[1] Dr. Parr expressed the same opinion more vigorously, declaring that "they were either written by Shakespeare or the Devil."

[2] This is William's version. According to Samuel's account, Boswell "with an extraordinary degree of rapture" said: "How happy I am to have lived to the present day of discovery of this glorious treasure. I shall now die in peace." Although William wrote some time after the event, his account is preferable for being so beautifully in character.

He could always flamboyantly stress a common opinion.

On February 25th, Dr. Parr and the most ardent of the believers took approval on the flood, and drew up a Certificate of Belief in the authenticity of the Papers. Twenty people signed, with Parr himself and Boswell (who again fell on his knees) taking the lead. The other eighteen signatories were John Tweddell, the archæologist, whose papers Lord Elgin is said to have stolen; the eccentric Radical Earl of Lauderdale, distinguished for appearing in the House "in the rough costume of Jacobinism"; Thomas Burgess; the Reverend James Scott; Samuel's great friend the Hon. John Byng; Baron Kinnaird; James Bindley of the Stamp Office; Sir Herbert Croft, whose *Love and Madness* was, in a sense, the inspiration of the papers he now acknowledged; the young Duke of Somerset; Henry Pye, the Poet Laureate; the Rev. Nathaniel Thornbury; Sir Isaac Heard, Garter King-of-Arms; Francis Webb, his secretary; John Hewlett, Biblical scholar, and translator of old records for the Common Pleas Office; John Pinkerton; Richard Valpy, Headmaster of Reading School, said to be the hardest flogger of his day; and Matthew Wyatt. Between them, they made a very fair cross-section of the culture of their time; William could hardly have hoped for a broader collection of dupes.

On the one side were Malone and some fellow commentators, a formidable but isolated group; a few scholars who doubted but dared not declare their disbelief;[1] and a handful of scurrilous

---

[1] Richard Porson, the Greek scholar, refused to sign the Certificate on the ground that he never subscribed to Professions of Faith, and, under the name of Samuel England, produced a Greek version of a nursery rhyme, which he claimed to be a newly discovered work of Sophocles. Joseph Ritson seems to have doubted the Papers, although, perhaps from hostility to Malone, he never openly said so. But neither of the pair made any public statement relating to the controversy.

journalists whose anonymity concealed their insignificance. Ranged against them was the solid phalanx of the believers, from the signatories of the Certificate, to Dr. Warton, Linley of the Drury Lane, Harris of Covent Garden, Burke, Pitt and the Prince of Wales. Seldom can an age so thoroughly have betrayed itself.

Chapter Six

THE HISTORICAL BACKGROUND

The eighteenth century prided itself on being the age of reason. Scientific criticism was developing; there was an increasing desire to know the objective truth, and a growing understanding of the methods by which it might be discovered. In medieval times a three-headed dog, an embassy from the East, or the report of a falling star in Bohemia, were all received with equal interest, given equal credence, and equally thought to have some metaphysical significance. In the eighteenth century wonders were examined critically, and taken seriously only in so far as they added to the general sum of knowledge.

Yet, at the same time, the age was astonishingly credulous, and its awakening caution was often its own betrayal. The old desire for marvels was now whetted by scientific curiosity; the gaper at raree-shows was touched with the ardour of a research-worker. Wonders might be examined scientifically, but if they passed an as yet elementary scrutiny their acceptance was all the more complete. The easy oddities of the past had been taken quite casually, as an amusement for the base and a symbol for the learned. The new extravagance was more important; passed by the expert, it became the evidence of some rare and valuable truth.

The eighteenth-century trickster had a more difficult task than his predecessors, but, if he succeeded, a more spectacular triumph. Mary Tofts of Godalming, who claimed to give birth to rabbits, had elaborately to feign conceptions and win the learned support of her local doctor before she was believed, but, once accepted as a genuine medical marvel, she won the widest celebrity, alarmed the pregnant ladies of the court and stirred Grub Street to its depths. Psalmanazar, too, who posed as a native of Formosa, and astonished Oxford with his cultural and geographical revelations, lived on fruit and raw herbs to support his pose, wore Formosan dress, and invented the language of his people down to written characters and a consistent grammar. None of his numerous predecessors in this sort of deception had had to be nearly so thorough, but none of them gained nearly so great a success.

In its eager curiosity the age was ready to welcome even exploded myths, and believed again the fabulous travellers' tales of previous centuries. One of the most persistent of these legends was that of the deadly Upas Tree. As early as the thirteenth century a travelling Friar had described this dangerous plant, and recounted in lurid detail how its sap rotted the flesh from the bones, and its poisonous scent slew beasts and vegetation for miles around. From that time onwards travellers made frequent references to the Upas Tree, and in 1666 it was a subject of debate before the Royal Society. The tales never varied very much, never contained first-hand descriptions of the tree's more astonishing properties, and were told and received with an ever-decreasing conviction.

In 1783 the fable flared up anew. In an article in the *London Magazine*, Försch, a surgeon from the Dutch East Indies, declared he had actually seen the tree, and described in polished and detailed narrative its appearance, situation, and the means by which its deadly sap was gathered. He had, he claimed, interviewed the worthy old priest who blessed the condemned prisoners sent to collect the juice, and obtained from him the first accurate information as to the nature and effects of the poison ever to be published in Europe. Försch's account of the Upas was more absurd and extraordinary but, at the same time, more soberly narrated than any of the earlier stories, and his article caused a great sensation. Erasmus Darwin included the Upas in his *Botanic Garden*,[1] the Batavian Society sent out a Committee of Investigation, and the curious public paid more attention to the story than ever before. The Upas legend was soon discredited by the learned, but not before it had gained enough credence to make it a popular metaphor.

Coincident with the growth of science was an increasing desire for accurate historical knowledge. As late as the seventeenth century, such a great translator as Philemon Holland could render Suetonius' reference to an Emperor's deification, as "canonised he was a saint in heaven," and, in spite of their wide classical reading, the Restoration dramatists were still careless of anachronism in their Greek or Roman dramas. By the middle of the eighteenth century this self-preoccupation was giving way; there was an eager if uninformed enthusiasm to learn the detail of the past, and Drury Lane presented costume pieces with painstaking attention to historical accuracy. Comparative criticism was developing; such "forgeries" as the accounts of the Trojan War by Dares the Phrygian and Dictys the Cretan, that passed as genuine in the Middle Ages, would not for a moment have deceived the Georgian scholar, any more than would the spurious Saxon

---

[1] *Fell* Upas *sits, the Hydra Tree of Death;*
Lo! from one root, the envenom'd soil below
A thousand vegetative serpents grow. . . .

Charter with which Westminster Abbey tricked Henry III. At the same time, this new knowledge of historical fact had not yet brought an accompanying sense of period, and there was little or none of that feeling for history that is the surest defence against fraud. With the canonical assurance of the enthusiastic amateur, historians stamped as irrefutably genuine everything whose falseness was not immediately obvious, and, having passed their judgment, defended an error for the credit of the science that made it.

George Steevens, the Shakespearian editor, could dupe the Society of Antiquaries with a piece of chimney-slab on which he had scratched in pseudo-runic characters: "Here King Hardcnut drank a wine-horn dry, stared about him, and died," because, with all their book-knowledge, the Antiquarians had no perception except in terms of their own age. History was either a lifeless pedantry or a contemporary scandal, and its students could detect only the most obvious of anachronisms. They always exposed deceptions in the end, but did so only by tracking down the technical errors that seem inevitable in even the most careful of fabrications, and destroying the evidence on which they had based their acceptance. To us, most of their pains seem wholly wasted; it took their whole critical apparatus to disprove a forgery that to-day would be dismissed at a glance. Historians had ceased to be content with the repetition of undocumented anecdotes, and were, for the first time, seeking direct evidence. Like the followers of every new science they made incredible blunders, and, working without precedents, were more easily deceived than their less conscientious predecessors. Their search for knowledge had all the blind eagerness of a passion; the age of reason was also the age of credulity.

Even so, the believers in the Shakespeare Papers should have had warning enough. Chatterton's forgeries were yet fresh in popular memory, and Macpherson, the "translator" of Ossian, was still living when Ireland published the first of his discoveries. There had even been Shakespearian fabrications earlier in the century; the oldest of William's readers must have heard of Theobald's *Edward III*, and aptly entitled *Double Falsehood*, or of Rowe's *Jane Shore*, which, though their claims were never taken very seriously, had caused a good deal of discussion at the time. But if the plays were too distant to stir recollection, Chatterton's manuscripts were not; for the Rowley Poems had aroused a storm that was not quite spent a quarter of a century after their author's death.

In a sense, William was actually helped by the forgeries of his predecessors. The Shakespeare Papers demanded comparison with the Rowley Manuscripts, and even their bitterest enemies were forced to admit that the precious relics emerged with great advantage. By William's time Chatterton-worship was at its height, and the dead poet was acclaimed a genius by the critics who had suppressed him during his life. One of his many biographers credited Chatterton with "the wild wit of Shakespeare, the sublime conceptions of Milton, and the long, resounding march of Dryden," and although this was probably an exceptional panegyric, it was fashionable to regard him as a poet of outstanding talent. The posthumous enhancement of Chatterton's abilities as a poet cast a reflected glamour on his skill as a forger, and he came to be considered the master-fabricator of English literature, as brilliant in deceit as he was in poetry. No one, it was thought, could succeed where such a genius had failed; any deception that seemed to surpass the

73

Rowley Manuscripts must, for that very reason, be no deception at all.

Actually, Chatterton's forgeries were exceedingly incompetent. He imitated ancient manuscripts as much from sentiment as from deceit, and his old parchments, smeared with yellow ochre and openly rubbed in the dirt of the street, can hardly have hoped to pass more than the most cursory examination. And if his technique was bad, Chatterton's language and style were still more unconvincing. In common with the serious scholars of his time he suffered from a crippling lack of reliable literary criticism, and found that accurate knowledge of medieval letters could only be acquired by a direct study for which he had neither means nor opportunity. He was forced to base his forgeries largely on Speght's Chaucer, and drew up a modern-medieval glossary from which he supplied the numerous obsolete words that gave the Rowley Poems their only show of antiquity. In phrasing, style and sentiment the poems were blatantly modern, and we find Chaucer's contemporary writing blank verse, pindaric odes, and such stanzas as:

> *Old Salnarville beheld hys son lie ded*
> *Against Erle Edelward his bowe-strynge drewe*
> *But Harold at one blowe made tweine his head*
> *He dy'd before the poignant arrowe flew.*
> *So was the hope of all the issue gone*
> *And in one battle fell the sire and son.*

Even in his use of antique words Chatterton often blundered. Apart from associating different dialects and periods, and using impossible forms for the tenses of verbs he knew only in the infinitive, he was sometimes drawn into appalling errors by the inadequacy of his glossary. Thus, in the *Battle of Hastings* he writes:

> *Itte whyzzd a ghastlie dynne in Normannes ear*
> *Then thundrying dyd upon hys Greave alyghte*
> *Pierce to his Hearte, and dyd hys Bowels tear.*

Presumably his word-list translated "greave" as "a piece of armour," without mentioning the part of the body on which it was worn.

Whatever their merits as poetry, the Rowley Poems are the worst of forgeries in which technical error is only exceeded by historical anachronism. But the romantic hero-worship that had grown up round Chatterton veiled the clumsy errors of his work, and sentimentality combined with forgetfulness to give the manuscripts a repute they had never enjoyed during their author's lifetime. Chatterton's readers, knowing in advance that the poems were spurious, lost sight of their weaknesses, and imagined the grossest of errors to be obvious only in the light of their own foreknowledge. The Shakespeare Papers came before a public that imagined it had already seen the best that a forger could do, and Ireland, by comparative superiority to an incompetent predecessor, gained for a time the weight of his rival's inflated reputation.

By comparison with his predecessors Ireland possessed a high degree of technical skill, and in the actual manufacture of his forgeries he showed an intelligence far in advance of his scanty historical knowledge. In the first place, nearly all his materials were quite genuine. The Lease and the other legal documents had been done on parchment cut from the ends of seventeenth-century deeds and conveyances, of which his employer had a plentiful supply. But most of the forgeries had to be written on old paper, and he had some difficulty in obtaining an adequate supply, until, for five shillings, an antique bookseller allowed him to cut the blank end-papers from all the sixteenth- and seventeenth-century quartos and folios in his stock. William always feared discovery through a water-mark, and whenever he used paper of uncertain age was careful to choose unmarked sheets, or those stamped only with the Jug, which a friend of his father had described as a typical Elizabethan device. The thread with which he tied together the bundles of smaller notes, he had torn from a frayed tapestry in the House of Lords when he went with his father to watch the King's robing; and, as we have seen, the braid that tied Willy's lock of hair was authentic enough to support its accompanying verses. Of all the materials used in preparing the manuscripts, the ink alone was modern; but, even so, its detection seems to have been quite beyond the chemistry of the period. The bitterest opponents of the Papers were forced to admit that their outward appearance at least was entirely convincing.

The writing and orthography of the manuscripts were a good deal easier to criticise, although here too detection is considerably simpler in the light of after-knowledge. Whenever William had a model to study in detail he could forge signatures with a fair degree of accuracy. He resorted to tracing only very occasionally, preferring to copy by eye or even from memory, and in consequence his copies resemble their originals closely and naturally but without showing slavish imitation. At first he tried carefully to reproduce the individual letters of Shakespeare's name in the body of the text, but after a while, as the pressure of work became heavier, he found no time for such painstaking copying, but dashed off the old hand as fast as he wrote his own. In the end, the Shakespearian hand became so natural to him that the writing on all the Papers bore a close mutual resemblance, and showed evident signs of being written with ease and rapidity. Since it was naturally assumed that forgery is a careful and laborious business, the opponents of the Papers found it difficult to explain away the spontaneity of the handwriting and the speed of the manuscripts' production, as it was obvious that the author wrote carelessly at a good speed, and had not drawn each separate word with the precision of a skilful forger. No one imagined the ease with which the antique hand could be written, and the hostile critics were forced to assume years of preparation to explain the full spate of discoveries. The handwriting might not look very Jacobean, but it did appear to be natural to its author.

But if there was some merit in the style of William's writing, there was none at all in his orthography. In spite of his fondness for old books, he had not the least idea of Elizabethan spelling, and clogged his forgeries with all the absurdities that had ruined his hero Chatterton. It is hard to understand how he reconciled the doubled vowels and multiplied consonants of his manuscripts with the relatively modern spelling of the quarto *Lear*, or what impelled him to repeat the endlessly emphasised errors of the Rowley Poems. Perhaps William could not clearly distinguish historical periods, and imagined that Shakespeare and Chaucer belonged to the same unchanging age; or perhaps his personal admiration for Chatterton had made him believe that his bogus-antique spelling was somehow intrinsically poetic. But whatever his motives, they effectively hastened his ruin; for the visual absurdity of his orthography gave rise to an unreasoned conviction of forgery, in precisely the same way that the visible

77

age of the Papers had at first proclaimed their authenticity.

It was their orthography that, more than any other single feature, finally overthrew the Forgeries, but a considerable time elapsed before it attracted really serious criticism. It must be remembered that the Papers were not published until over a year after their first discovery; before that time they could be viewed only at Mr. Ireland's house under strict supervision, with little opportunity of taking notes or making a transcript. Very few of the worshipping visitors can have been able themselves easily to decipher the documents, and when William or his father declaimed the choicer passages to a circle of admirers it is very unlikely that they stressed the oddities of the spelling. Even those few who could actually read the originals would probably not have noticed its full enormity. The orthography must have combined with the sprawling obscurity of the writing to invest the sense with the mysterious importance of a barely transliterated cipher, and the fantastic spelling of the manuscripts have seemed as little related to ordinary standards as were the faded ink, or the stained and crumbling parchment on which the Papers were written. Part of the rapturous joy the discoveries at first excited may have arisen from the instinct that finds such peculiar pleasure in detecting a glimmer of sense in an uncomprehended inscription. In spite of the furore excited by the Papers, no one save Samuel and a few of his closest friends had studied them in any detail before they were printed and published. It had originally been intended to publish the Manuscripts *after* the performance of *Vortigern,* and had Samuel been able to do so the story of the forgeries might well have been very different. But, as we shall see, fortune began to desert him.

To the modern mind, a strong reason for rejecting the Papers was the peculiar circumstance of their reported discovery. The strange secrecy of the Mysterious Gentleman, and the incredible profusion of his Shakespearian manuscripts, would seem sufficient to arouse the most serious doubts, if not a complete disbelief of the whole story.

In 1795 no one, not even the most relentlessly hostile, ventured to commit themselves to such a position. On the face of things, there seemed nothing especially unusual in the attitude of Mr. H. Here was a gentleman of wealth, and probably rank, who had given some valuable papers to a young man to whom he had taken a fancy. Those who demanded to be told his name and identity never maintained they had any right to the knowledge, but merely suggested that in these particular circumstances it would be a fair and generous act to come forward and acknowledge original ownership. It is significant that no one argued that such an action would win the Gentleman any credit; in so doing he would simply have helped his young friend at some slight expense of personal dignity. When Mr. H. refused to reveal himself he displayed neither eccentricity nor dishonesty, but merely a rather old-fashioned sense of the dignity due to his station. None of the opposition seriously blamed him for preserving his secrecy; they were perfectly well aware of their own vindictive scurrility, and quite understood the unwillingness of a man of position to risk being slandered by pamphlets and daily journals. Samuel himself felt a little aggrieved at the Gentleman's behaviour, but the world admitted that he had acted with perfect propriety.

Nor was there anything especially suspicious in the extent

and importance of the Papers. The latter part of the eighteenth century was an age of remarkable documentary discoveries. For the first time records were being scientifically checked, old texts properly criticised, and the priceless, neglected libraries of country houses searched and catalogued in the conscious hope of finding literary treasure. Amateur and professional scholars were continually making discoveries of less popular interest, perhaps, than that of the Ireland Papers, but of equal extent and in equally curious fashion; and a considerable part of our surviving manuscript records were first collected and preserved during Samuel Ireland's lifetime. Albany Wallis, Samuel's neighbour in Norfolk Street, had found in 1768 the Mortgage Deed of Shakespeare's property in Blackfriars, and he further discovered a Conveyance of the same property actually during the course of William's forgeries. Of all possible treasure-trove, Shakespeariana was the most desirable and, so it seemed, not the least improbable of discovery. For a man of his great contemporary and posthumous reputation Shakespeare had left astonishingly little personal record, and many accounted for the disappearance of the poet's papers by the supposition that they had all been gathered together in one place by a friend or relative and never allowed to disperse. It was widely believed that such papers must still be extant, and the public was ready to accept the most extensive of windfalls in the most uncritical spirit. When William brought forward the first of the forgeries, Samuel immediately asked him whether there were others, and accepted with increasing belief each further addition to the bulk of the manuscripts. So far from requiring conviction against its will, the literary public was almost expecting the Shakespeare Papers.

Many facts conspired to aid William's deception. In the first place, there was only a faulty co-ordination of knowledge; private individuals possessed unique historical documents of which there might well be neither facsimile nor transcript, so that a personal difference between scholars could often hinder or even prohibit important research. Beyond a small but vociferous circle there seems to have been, even in the literary world, a curious lack of interest in the discovery. It is not surprising that the charwoman who cleaned William's office should have been ignorant of the controversy, and merely remark, when she watched him forge one of the letters, that he could do "unaccountable strange things"; but it seems almost incredible that he could openly purchase materials for forgery without exciting comment. "At a period when the public mind was occupied with the Shakespeare papers," William notes in his *Confessions*, "and the daily newspapers teemed with paragraphs on the subject; when I was in the middle of my career, my ink failed me; and although hazardous the procedure, I positively applied to the very same journeyman in Mr. Laurie's shop, who for a shilling prepared a second bottle of the beforementioned ink; which circumstance was never mentioned either by Mr. Laurie or his workman, although the fame of the manuscripts was perfectly well known to them, and that I was the person supposed to have discovered them." Still stranger than Mr. Laurie's indifference seems the daring or idiocy that impelled William to take so extraordinary a risk.

The basic cause for the Papers' acceptance lay in the nature of their contents. The ancient appearance of the manuscripts was enough to command a reasonable belief in their authenticity;

but it was their feeling, outlook and emotional attitude that aroused the passionate adoration that distinguishes the Ireland Forgeries from the deceptions that preceded and followed them.

With all its new respect for the past and worship for the literary genius of previous ages, the late eighteenth century retained enough of the Augustan critical spirit to deplore the crudity of ancient literature while admiring its distant fire. One of the many admirers of Ossian compares him favourably with Homer, on the ground that his Celtic heroes treat the bodies of their fallen enemies with gentlemanly sentimentality, instead of with the mockery and mutilation favoured by their Homeric prototypes; and it is typical of the time that the writer includes such an instance of Ossian's humaneness as part of his poetic merit. While the past was held in increasing respect, there was no tendency to regard it as a Golden Age— the eighteenth-century man reserved that honour for his own epoch—and while it was admitted that history had mountains overshadowing the puny present, yet most of the past was valley and swamp, unwarmed by the steady sun of reason and wanting the healthy breeze of critical good taste. Shakespeare was undoubtedly a giant, with all a giant's grandeur and strength; but he also exhibited the tactless grossness of such huge creatures, and sometimes, at his most sublime moments, would exhibit a disturbing lack of taste and refinement. Garrick had done more than anyone to enhance Shakespeare's name and restore his glories to public recognition; yet the same man that had organised the Stratford Jubilee could re-write *King Lear* to suit the superior taste of his own time, and provide an ending in which Cordelia marries Edgar, and Lear, Kent and

Gloucester live happily together ever after.[1] This sort of alteration was by no means uncommon, and John Philip Kemble, who was to play the lead in *Vortigern*, presented a production of the *Comedy of Errors* in which the Dromios were blackamoor clowns.

When William produced his forgeries these two elements of Shakespeare-worship and Shakespeare-emendation were still in conflict, and the compromise of letting Shakespeare amend himself was received with a joy that must have been strongly tinted with relief. The Believers found the last blots on their idol wiped away by his own hand, and the Bard stood forth as grand in taste as he was in the cruder stuff of genius. "These papers," wrote one supporter, "show him in a moral and religious point of view, as amiable, tender and pleasing as his other Works show him pre-eminent, great and wonderful. They exhibit him full of Friendship, Benevolence, Pity, Gratitude and Love. The milk of human kindness flows as readily from his pen as do his bold and sublime Descriptions"; while another, more succinctly, observed that "they served to raise the moral character of the divine poet as high in my veneration as his genius was before." The sentimental absurdities that seem most to betray the forgeries were really their strongest recommendation, and instead of noticing the anachronism, their readers observed with delight that Shakespeare, after all, was

[1] The whole play was re-written, but the ending, of course, required the most creative work.

"*Lear:* But Edgar, I defer thy joys too long,
      Thou serv'st distressed Cordelia, take her crown'd
      Th' imperial grace fresh blooming on her brow.
      Nay, Gloucester, thou hast here a father's right
      Thy helping hand t'heap blessings on their heads.
Kent: Old Kent throws in his hearty wishes too."

really one of themselves. William, in fact, was the subtlest of unconscious sycophants, and had borrowed the popular idol to flatter popular taste. Is it surprising that he found so many supporters?

Finally, caution recommended belief in the Discoveries. Worship of the past was now the rule, and there was no writer living with reputation enough to attack the famous dead. The believers in the Papers knew that the penalty for a mistake could only be a few jeers and a dozen slanderous paragraphs forgotten as soon as read; the memory of their duping would only endure until the next deception. But if the Papers *were* proved genuine, those who had opposed them would be utterly ruined, for the public would never forgive, and their enemies never forget, the inexpiable sin of denying and insulting the sacred. For this reason the few who publicly avowed their scepticism were far more active than the numerous supporters, since they knew that failure to disprove the Manuscripts meant disgrace for themselves and the end of their reputation. To believe in a forgery was a laughable stupidity; to mock at Shakespeare's intimate papers was downright blasphemy. To accept the Discoveries was to play for safety.

Chapter Seven

THE MYSTERIOUS GENTLEMAN

The immediate acceptance of the Forgeries and the absurd adulation that was poured on their supposed author threw William Ireland partly off his balance. He had always suffered from a deep sense of inferiority, and the self-conceit that finally led him to his elaborate deception was but a shallow defence against his father's painfully obvious contempt. His pathetic efforts to convince himself of his own genius were the weakest of wish-fulfilments, and a fearful respect for Samuel's learning made him so outwardly dull that even his own family thought him wholly untalented. It is impossible to exaggerate the change wrought in him by the Papers' reception. His first published works, for that was what the Forgeries amounted to, were received not merely as genuine, but as writings of extreme genius; and praised not only by antiquarian scholars, but by poets, writers and literary critics. William had hoped for acceptance and received complete adoration. Can he be blamed for losing his head?

For the first few weeks of his new importance William could not suppress his excitement, and regaled the family with wild stories of the treasures shortly to be revealed; it was at this time that he described the seal and portraits of Shakespeare that were afterwards to cause him so much trouble. But his greatest delight was to tell of the Gent's kindness and munificence, and show in the noble generosity of his patron a reflected image of his own extraordinary merits. Mr. H. (as the Gent. now called himself) was not content to be casually open-handed, but legally sealed his benevolence with a Deed, specially drawn up by the Attorney-General, by which William received all future discoveries relative to Shakespeare, with the sole proviso that the document be kept always under lock and key, lest others pry into the secret of the donor's identity. Mr. H. kept his promises; for when an equally mysterious friend wrote offering two thousand pounds to search through his chest of old papers, he referred the decision to William, saying that should he accept he might keep the money for himself. William indignantly refused to part with the sacred relics, and when the would-be purchaser called in person to offer a further five hundred pounds, Mr. H., "ringing the bell, ordered the servant to show him downstairs with all speed."[1]

To all these tales the family listened with eager attention, and William, for the first time in his life, found himself the centre of respect and admiration. He began to cultivate a portentous secretiveness varied by the wild humours of another Chatterton, until his father and sisters came to treat him with the careful respect due to an important stranger.

On Samuel, the enthusiastic welcome afforded the Manuscripts had rather a different effect. As soon as he recovered from his first joy and astonishment, he began to be faintly perturbed; the Discoveries were on a far larger scale than he had imagined possible, and called for a fuller account of their origin than the curiously vague explanation that had accompanied the Fraser Lease. William's extraordinary stories of his

[1] William afterwards realised he had made a mistake in telling this anecdote, for if the Gent's secrecy was so inviolable, how did it happen that some other person knew about the Papers? He therefore changed his story, and said he believed the manuscripts the purchaser sought were not Shakespearian, but to do with some landed property.

reclusive friend, and, still more, the non-appearance of the promised seal and portraits, worried Samuel, and he began to question his son more closely about the Mysterious Gentleman. He trusted William, as much from belief in his stupidity as from faith in his honesty, yet cooler reflection showed the oddity of the story, and made him realise that his friends would expect, and his enemies demand, a more detailed statement as to the source of the Papers.

William proved most difficult to question, and resisted the cross-examination of Samuel and his friends with displays of temperamental resentment that were not altogether assumed for the occasion. "Your son, yesterday, walked home with me," reported one amateur investigator, "when I touched gently (further will not do I find) upon the wonder of the discovery; the history of the donor and upon his *strange drawback*; and all the *mystery* of his *delays*. All that I could draw from him was that the *Gentleman* had given him *much*; would give him *all*. That he had no thoughts of withholding them from you— that you should direct and guide him; that when he brought them some evenings ago he could not keep them longer. . . .

". . . . In short, I perceive, you must be *calm* with him— coax him—give him his *own way*, and trust to Nature. My only fear is that he may be seized by some artful man—to his defraud and to your prejudice. . . . I must repeat to you—that your conduct to your son (in this business) must be slow and temperate; else he may dash forth."

But neither questioning, urging nor persuading could pierce William's guarded garrulity, and Samuel resolved himself to write to the mysterious Gent. at the earliest opportunity. It was not long before he found an excuse. His *Picturesque Views*

of the Warwickshire Avon, in preparation for which he had made
the journey to Stratford, was now ready for the press, and
he decided to refer in the Preface to the discovery of the
Papers:

"If in the pages of this volume he [the author] may be
thought in the smallest degree to have elucidated any circumstance of Shakespeare's life, or any passage in the noble effusions
of his more than human mind, his utmost pride and wish is
fully gratified . . . he has the means . . . at a future day to
present a picture of that mind, which no one has ever presumed
to copy, an entire Drama! yet unknown to the world, in his
own handwriting."

It was only courteous to send a proof copy to Mr. H. and
ask his permission to make the reference. What could be
more proper than, at the same time, tactfully to remind him
of the promised full-length portrait, and pointedly promise to
respect his secrecy? On January 31st, 1795, Samuel gave his
son the letter and the proofs, with strict instructions to deliver
them immediately to his patron.

William had a wonderful opportunity and he used it to the
full. In a beautifully neat hand, resembling his usual untidy
scrawl only in omitting the punctuation, he replied to his
father with warmth and dignity:

The perusal of your preface has I assure you been produc-
tive of the greatest pleasure and satisfaction and the genteel
manner in which it was offered adds still more to the gratification I have received . . . but for the portrait (though *I
assure you* your son shall have it) for particular reasons as yet I
wish to keep secret, but I may even say more it is a delicate
business which remains alone in the bosom of your son for I

will frankly own all he has yet said has been with my concurrence but he is acquainted with much more which I trust
and am assured he has never mentioned.

It may appear strange that a young man like myself
should have thus formed a friendship for one he has so little
knowledge of, but I do assure you *Dr. sir* without flattery he
is a young man after *my own heart* in whom I would confide
and even consult on the nicest affair. In spring (with joy I
say it) I shall hope for the Pleasure of seeing him, when I do
assure you all shall be his own. As he seems to speak much
of the Lear for *you*, and for which I still esteem him more
and more, you shall in a short time have it not from *me* but
through his hands. . . . Pray excuse my familiarity but I
cannot write otherwise to the father of one whom I esteem. . . .

Samuel was delighted with such friendly condescension, and
William with his usual impetuosity wrote again on the following day with a suggestion he had long cherished but dared
not make in perso...

"Excuse the liberty I have taken in addressing you a second
time," wrote Mr. H. urgently, "it is merely to let you know
the particular desire I have that your son should take himself
one of the parts in the new play. He has hinted to me what
passed between you this evening, and I think the change will
be for the better— Should you wish at any time to communicate anything to me, I shall be always sure of receiving it
through the hands of my Dear young friend. . . ."

This was a critical test of Samuel's respect for his correspondent. He had always been accustomed to regard his son as
nearly worthless, and, in the ordinary way, would have contemptuously denied him any share of dramatic talent. Mr.
H.'s interest made Samuel regard the matter in a new light,

and after a few days hesitation he replied with the suggestion that William should appear for one night only, "making that night sacred only to Shakespeare, and to introduce all the characters in a [pageant] after the play." Never before had he made such a concession to his son's abilities, and from that day Mr. H. became spokesman of William's secret ambitions. Requests he dared not make and conceits he feared to express could safely be left to his powerful patron, for whose casual word Samuel had more attention than for his son's most earnest entreaty. As months passed the Gentleman bothered ever less to prove the authenticity of the Papers, but stressed more and more the genius of the youth who had discovered them.

In the first flush of his new assurance William was absurdly indiscreet, and we find him skittishly attacking prejudices that his father held sacred even from wealthy and influential gentlemen:

> . . . I saw my young friend yesterday morning; we spoke on the subject of the new taxing. I was surprised by what he said to find you a friend of the Ministry, when by what he has always told me I thought you of the minority. You must allow that all who contribute their guineas for Powder give money for the support of the war, and as I have never been a friend to it in any one Instance neither will I in this, I do assure you on my Honour. My hair is now combed to its real colour and will remain hanging loosely on my shoulders 'that Ladys may now perfume it with their balmy kisses.' Besides, you cannot be an enemy to the manner in which our *Willy* wore his hair. Let me I beseech you see your son with flowing locks, it is not only manly but showing yourself averse to bloodshed. I should not ever request to see you yourself out of powder, but, however, your son I should lay a stress on, as he also seems to wish it.

This was going a little too far. Mr. H. commanded respect by his wealth and generosity, but such an attempt to interfere with parental discipline, and, still more, the sprightly bad taste of the reference to *Willy*, seem to have offended Samuel, and he declined to answer the letter. The Gent. must have heard of his displeasure, for he hastened to make amends by promising to have the manuscript of *Lear* enclosed in a rare and curious binding. But, after a time, William persuaded him to let Samuel himself have it bound in russia with gilt clasps.

Samuel had not entered into correspondence in order to exchange compliments, or to be advised about his son's coiffure, and on March 3rd he wrote to Mr. H. telling him of the proposed publication of the manuscripts, and asking his help in writing the Preface. For the first time he explained the difficulty of his situation, and definitely requested further information as to the source and history of the Shakespeare Papers:

> . . . of the genuineness there cannot be a shadow of doubt in the mind of the candid—but I shall have to do with some, I fear, not of that class—Do you not think they will be apt to say that although the Deeds and Theatrical Papers and even the Plays might with much propriety have fallen into the hands of John Hemings his very intimate friend, and who succeeded him in the management of the theatre, yet it cannot with the same propriety be admitted that letters to his wife, his Profession of Faith, and other circumstances of a domestic nature, should have gone with them, but that they remained with his wife . . . [*very obscure*] . . . the critics may be inclined to say—to all this we have only Mr. Ireland's assertions—and therefore we will still doubt and require further explanation. . . . I do not wish in any degree to be

understood in any manner desiring to make use of your name, on the contrary, it shall remain inviolate with me till death if required—my wish is merely to have your concurrence in every step I take. I yet flatter myself that I may one day have the happiness and honour of personally being acquainted with the Gent. who is with so much sincerity the friend of my son, and who is being the restorer of so invaluable a treasure to the public mind as the papers of our immortal Shakespeare. . . .

William was at a loss. The questions were reasonable and insistent, and could not easily be evaded by flattery or dissimulation. He tried to appease his father by telling him that Mr. H. intended to preserve the manuscript of *Vortigern* in an iron case "which was to be covered," as Samuel noted in his day-book, "with crimson velvet and studded with gold, and Shakespeare's arms was to be embroidered on one side and my son's on the other, and that the binding was to cost the Gent. twenty pounds." But flattering though this be it was not what Samuel wanted, and six weeks later he again wrote to the dilatory H., this time in rather stronger terms:

DEAR SIR,

Not having been favoured with an answer to my last letter written many weeks since, it was not my intention again to have intruded on you, but the delicate and painful situation in which I now stand before the public urges me strongly to address you on the subject. You once flattered me with the hope that I should one day have the favour of becoming acquainted with a Gent. to whom I owed so much, from the high gratification received from his liberality. This, it seems, I am denied—and consequently am deprived of laying before the public any authority as to the originality of the Papers—

I requested my son to inform you of the plan that suggested itself, from which some satisfaction might be derived to the Public, and yet your name, if necessary, might remain concealed. I am sorry to say, Sir, that myself and my family are now so involved and implicated in the business that something is absolutely necessary to be done, and that immediately, or the consequences may be fatal. I beg to [? ?] to you that, as you promised me in your last, a number of Documents should be brought forth, not only papers, but pictures, drawings etc., that the latter articles would be particularly interesting and might, as being a new specimen of evidence, tend in a great measure to give authenticity to the Papers, and thereby give relief to the mind of an oppressed family—In short, Sir, I submit the business to your mature consideration, and request that you will determine on something that may terminate the anxiety of all parties—I beg to inform you that my situation as to future advantages is likewise at stake as I have now a work ready to lay before the public that has cost me a considerable sum of money, which I dare not bring forward on account of the odium I now labour under from being possessed of the Shakespeare MSS. in so ambiguous and mysterious a manner as to render their authenticity totally [? ?]. Again, Sir, I request a favourable construction may be put on the request contained in this letter, and that you will speedily determine on some mode to alleviate the state of mind and feelings of, Dr. Sir,

yours etc.
SAMUEL IRELAND

William found himself in a very difficult position. There was no possible way of answering his father's natural insistence, and each day the Gentleman failed to reply lowered Samuel's good opinion of his manners and honesty. For a time William tried tentatively to withdraw the more impossible of his promises, and began to admit exaggeration in his descriptions of future discoveries. Many of the treasures he once claimed to have seen he now said were contained only in a list of the relics made by Mr. H.'s ancestor, and might well have been lost or destroyed, since "the Gent. remembered when a child having seen some parcels of Papers exactly like those now remaining, carried down for use to a certain place in the garden." But no latter-day evasion of his previous promises could explain away such objects as the full-length portrait which William had so fully described, and soon he found himself obliged to satisfy his father, or for ever to destroy his useful respect for the Gentleman. The only hope was to appeal to Samuel's vanity and divert his inconstant attention to some flattering red-herring.

On June 12th (soon after he presented the Deed of Gift) William told his father of a remarkable discovery that at last clearly proved the ancient descent of the family of Ireland. Searching through an old chest at the Gentleman's country house, he had chanced on an illuminated manuscript of the fifteenth century, with a picture of King Henry V presenting a banner to a kneeling knight. Underneath was written, "Ireland, thou hast deserved well for thy valor, and shalt have a part of our Arms of England for thy bravery." Ireland, continued the manuscript, had modestly protested his unworthiness of so signal an honour, but the king had replied, "Thou shalt have a bloody coat besprinkled with the Arms of France." The document, William said, was endorsed by each successive Ireland, beginning:

"I Arthur Ireland had this awarded me at Agincourt by Henry the 5th, 1418 [*sic*].

"I Montgomery Henry Ireland had this at my father's death, 1430," and so on through,

"I Edward James Henry Ireland had this at my brother's death who was killed in France by his favourite horse, 1499," down to Shakespeare's friend, William Henry Ireland, who had received it on his father's death in 1567.

Nothing could have been better calculated to allay Samuel's suspicions. His obscure beginnings had made him a social snob, and his delight in the Shakespeare Papers lay, partly at least, in the easy introduction they afforded to the wealthy and titled. He fancied himself of ancient, if not of noble, blood, and was greatly disappointed when even Sir Isaac Heard and his other friends among the Heralds had been unable to trace the grant of his coat of arms. This latest discovery fed Samuel's fondest ambition, and joy at such wonderful proof of his ancient lineage made him quite forget his growing distrust of the Gentleman.

But, though he was immediately successful, William had seriously overreached himself. When first he described the Grant and made a rough sketch of its illuminations, he intended actually to produce the original, realising, perhaps, that his father would eagerly welcome the crudest of forgeries. But when he sought a genuine signature of Henry V in order to make a copy, he found, to his dismay, that nothing was known to exist in the king's handwriting. He dared not invent a signature, for were a genuine specimen ever discovered it would at once overturn not only the Grant, but the whole of the Shakespeare Manuscripts. Better to suffer his father's displeasure than risk the ruin of the entire project.

Samuel's patience was soon exhausted by the evasiveness of his son, and early in July he directly approached Mr. H.:

My impatience to view the grant of Arms, which I had several times hinted to my son, you will no doubt excuse, as it is a kind of personal gratification that would not be unnatural to any of us. I beg at the same time you may not hasten the delivery of it till you have fully made every use of it you intended. . . . Permit me again to request of your acquaintance, and that you will do me the favour of taking a family drive with us before you quit town. . . .

Mr. H. did not at once reply, but thanked Mr. Ireland through his son, and promised him a beautiful writing-desk, with a "curious mechanism" and a "stain'd leather cover lined with green Baize." This was the first time the Gent. had directed his famed liberality towards the father of his young friend, and Samuel must have dreamt of a wonderful future in which the munificent H. restored the ancient House of Ireland to its former glories. For the moment he was in high good humour, and William dared to express the secret conviction that had grown in him from the earliest days of the Forgeries. Whether he had long intended to do so and at last judged the moment secure, or whether he was inflamed by a propitious instant is hard to determine. In any event, towards the end of July, Mr. H. informed Samuel that his son was a genius:

For some time back it has been my wish to give you a letter unknown to your son. In doing this I assure you I break my promise, and therefore must beg, nay insist, on the strictest secrecy from you. As his father I think it but right that you should know by what he often tells me is in general thought of him. The contents, I am conscious, of this letter will not a little astonish you, and I myself must equally confess myself lost in wonder. He tells me he is in general look'd upon as a young man that scarce knows how to write a good letter— you yourself shall be the judge by what follows—I have now before me part of a *Play* written by *your son* which for style and greatness of thought is equal to any one of Shakespeare's. Let me intreat you, Dr. sir, not to smile, for on my honour it is most true.

He has chosen the subject of Wm. the Conqueror, and tells me he intends writing a series of plays to make up with Shakespeare's a complete history of the Kings of England. He wishes it to remain unknown, therefore I again rely on your honour in this affair. It must appear strange why I should have taken so particular a liking to him. His extra-ordinary talents would make anyone partial—I often talk with him and never before found one even of twice his age that knew so much of human nature. Do not think this flattery, for I again vouch to the truth of my assertion. *No man* but your *son* ever wrote like *Shakespeare*. This is bold, I confess, but it is true. He often says he knows learning will not make a *Poet*, neither will he look to any author. He often told me his blood boils a little when he is [held?] a silly young man, but still he is determined to remain secret. I have read what he has written of the Play and got him to give me the enclosed speech copied by himself from the original. I promised him I never would show it but told him I wanted to keep it for myself, on these conditions he gave it to me; it is not a chosen one I assure you, but *you* may judge of the [style] and grandeur of thought and then ask if it is not close on the heels of Shakespeare. It was originally composed in my room and in the writing he made but three blurs, but wished to make alterations. I begged to have it from the rough copy which is just as you find it. He never comes in to me but instantly notes down everything that has struck him in his walk. I have frequently asked where he can get such thoughts, all the answer he makes is this 'I borrow them from nature.' I also enquired why he wishes to be secret, to which he says 'I desire to be thought to know but little.' Let me beg you to examine him closely; you will find what I advance is but the truth. He likewise often says his mind *loathes* the confined *dingdong* study of the law, and yet says he will remain quiet till a proper opportunity. He has a large ledger in which as I may say he chronicles everything that strikes him and from this he forms his speeches. He told me he took the enclosed from walking alone in Westminster Abbey.

Mr. I—upon my honour and soul I would not scruple giving £2,000 a year to have a son with such extraordinary facilities. If at *twenty* he can write so what will he do hereafter. The more I see of him the more I am amazed. If your *son* is not a second Shakespeare I am not a *man*. Keep this to yourself, do not even mention it to any soul living, only mark well what I have here told you. I will not give you the *Inventory* now as it would seem very strange to him, but will make him the bearer as usual. . . .

I remain Dr. sir,

H.

Put a seal upon your lips to all that has passed, but Remember these words.

Your *son* is brother in genius to Shakespeare. He is the only man that ever walked with him hand in hand.

Enclosed with this letter was a poem. Earl Edwyn is musing in the porch of Westminster Abbey:

> *O my good Lord how lingering passed the time*
> *Whilse in yon porch I did wait your coming*
> *Yet as this Cloistral Arch this bright heaven*
> *Doth shine upon the Emerald tipt wave*
> *And paints upon the deep each passing cloud*
> *E'ene so the smallest and most gentle Plant*
> *That waves fore the breath of thee sweet heaven*

To man gives food for contemplation
And shows how soon this blazing flame of youth
Must sink on Age's chilling Icy Bed
And dwindle down to second nothingness. . . .

Then the Earl rebukes the Abbey:

Indeed at best thou'rt but a slaughter house
Throwing thy lines to catch the minds of Men
Bedecking them with Robes of gilded Pomp
Blowing in their ears the feverous blast
Of mirth, feasts, merriment, Prosperity,
Then on a sudden grappling with their souls
Thou knittest them at once to death eterne.

Samuel was delighted by this unexpected evidence of his son's talents, and replied immediately in the warmest terms:

Your letter has given me infinite pleasure—I have read the lines enclosed in it, and that with a degree of astonishment I cannot express, as I assure you it is the first specimen of my son's poetical talents I have ever seen. If I have ever found reason to complain of his want of information it has been from an affectionate attention towards him, and an eagerness to promote his application to certain authors from whom I was convinced he might receive information. Your good opinion of him weighs strongly on my mind, and I am happy that he has fallen into the hands of such a friend. . . .

But he was not so overwhelmed with the Gent's revelations that he forgot his preoccupying curiosity:

. . . There is indeed, Sir, but one circumstance attending your friendship towards him that gives me pain, and that is my being so total a stranger to one to whom I owe so much.

If it is your wish to remain unknown to the Public, may I without intrusion on your friendship request to have an interview on the most private ground imaginable. You think he can keep a secret, and I think he can; but my experience in life will, I flatter myself, certainly enable me to be equally secret if required. I lay the more stress on this matter, as it certainly appears strange to the world that my son at his age is entrusted to the knowledge of such a friendship, while I am kept totally in a state of suspense. I here pledge my honour that no one person in the world shall know more than they know at present—but it is for my own gratification that I say so much, and I flatter myself that for a moment placing yourself in the situation in which I now stand—which has become a public one from your liberality—you would think much as I do on the subject. If I have said too much, pardon my request, and do not deem it an impertinent curiosity, but rather one that arises from a grateful respect to yourself, and an affectionate regard to my son. I thank you for the Deed of Gift, and for your intention of sending me the schedule of all the Documents that are to come forth— amongst which permit me again to mention the grant of Arms, which if it should come before the Court in Doctors Commons will be a material object to proceed on, and without which I cannot, as I am informed, take any practical steps to [insure] a property in the Papers, and consequently cannot prepare the preface nor the work for the public eye. I should esteem the favour of a speedy answer. . . .

But William had no patience with his father's enquiries, and devoted himself to the public display of his newly admitted genius. In the first flush of his open pride he seems to have quarrelled with his family and countered their rebukes with the Gent's praises; for five days later we find Mr. H. writing to Samuel in a tone of dignified penitence, and painting

William as suffering Chatterton rather than triumphant Shakespeare:

> . . . Your son has enquired what letter *I* had written to you, but I have evaded his curiosity. He has written a good deal since my last, and even cried like a child because the pains in his head would not permit him to apply as he wished. If the specimen which I sent afforded pleasure what would be your feelings in receiving things superior in every degree. Indeed Mr. I. you must be completely happy. He has told me you talk a great deal to him now, and tells me he hopes I have not blab'd. . . . I long Mr. I. you will not conceive that I have a wish to restrain any advice on your part to your son—were I so to act I should greatly [impugn] your knowledge of the world and take upon myself to tutor where I should rather *myself* look for *Information*. I only mentioned what he had often *laughingly* told me. He has ever said much about his own disposition, but says he cannot account for his warmth of *temper*. But with regard to yourself and all those most dear to him he never utters a syllable unbecoming a dutiful and loving son. O Mr. I.—pray look upon yourself, happy in having a son *who if he lives* must make futurity amazed. . . .

At last Samuel realised the vanity of further questioning. Mr. H. was not to be drawn; whatever his secret might be he meant to conceal it, and would give no answer either to pleading or protest. Much as he desired his son to win wealthy patrons, Samuel rapidly tired of the Gentleman's endless praises and decided to drop the correspondence. There must surely be other means of learning the hidden truth.

During the following months Samuel followed every futile line of enquiry that hope or despair suggested. Report of his investigation spread, and friends, acquaintances, and some who were neither, offered their advice and invariably fruitless assistance. The most hopeful clue was provided by a Mr. Pope, a self-professed student of topographical history, who called at Norfolk Street with a long story of a Mr. Hodges who had formerly claimed to possess Shakespeare's plays in the original manuscript. Research revealed, according to Mr. Pope, that the papers were now in the hands of a Lady Hammond, whose address, unfortunately, was unknown, but who would surely not be difficult to trace. And so the pursuit went on, with Mr. Pope gradually fading from the picture until at last he wholly disappeared, and a friend wrote to Samuel: "I have made enquiry about the person you mentioned, and find that he left his lodgings *without paying*, and is not to be found."

By November the matter was urgent. The promised volume of *Miscellaneous Papers . . . under the hand and seal of William Shakespeare* was nearly ready for the press, and its preface demanded an account of the Papers' origin. Samuel questioned and threatened his son with such persistence that William was finally forced into a course he had long avoided, and sought the help of his friend Montague Talbot, the only other person who knew the real origin of the Discoveries.

Chapter Eight

MONTAGUE TALBOT

William Ireland and Montague Talbot had been friendly long before the beginning of the Forgeries. Talbot, like William, was articled to a conveyancer, and the pair, finding an exchange of visits and conversation far pleasanter than eight hours of solitary idleness in their respective offices, soon struck up a friendship, and before long Talbot became a frequent visitor to Norfolk Street. In almost everything save a common dislike of the Law the friends were wholly dissimilar. Talbot was a gay, handsome, dashing young man, whose easy ambitions lay behind the footlights rather than in a Court of Law; and Mrs. Freeman found his friendly gallantries far more attractive than the reclusive dullness of the moody son of the house. Although he had certain literary leanings and, as was the fashion of the time, fancied himself as a minor poet, Talbot was quite insensitive to William's imaginative love of the past and delighted to mock at his slightly affected antiquarianism. It is hard to see what actually kept them together. Perhaps William admired the other's verve and confidence, while Talbot, himself essentially slow-witted, had a secret respect for his friend's superior intellect. At any rate, they were on the best of terms, and when Talbot left his office in 1794 in order to follow his "favourite pursuit" of the stage, he was still William's most intimate friend.

William forged the first of the Papers while the other was out of town; else, as he says, he would never have been allowed the undisturbed opportunity; and when Talbot returned to

London he found the Shakespearian sensation at its height and his bookish friend the centre of learned attention. As soon as he called at Norfolk Street the Papers were proudly shown to him, and in spite of their antique appearance he immediately suspected William's handiwork, although William himself strongly denied their authorship, and remained firm under private questioning and public insinuation. But Talbot was not the man to be put off so easily, and for the next few days he made a practice of paying unexpected visits to his friend's chambers in the hope of catching him unawares. At first William was very cautious, and worked facing a window which commanded the only entrance to his office, but at last Talbot, creeping bent double close to the wall, got to the door unobserved, "darted into the Chambers," and seized William's hand as he tried to conceal a half-finished manuscript. There was nothing to do but let him into the secret.

At first Talbot had little to do with the forgeries. He was no antiquarian, and lacked both the imagination to conceive the Papers and the skill with which to execute them, while his frequent absences from town put active co-operation out of the question. William had admitted him to the secret only under compulsion, and was exceedingly thankful to find that his friend did not wish to help in the work, but merely to enjoy the vicarious excitement of sharing another's adventure.

Talbot found the deception a source of endless amusement, and demanded to be kept constantly informed of each move in William's campaign against scholarship. His was the rather childish idea that their letters should be written in code, by means of "a sheet of paper having several pieces cut from different parts of it; which, when desirous of writing, was placed on a piece of post paper; when the communication to be made was written on the parts of the post paper appearing through the holes so made in the mutilated sheet; after which the blanks left were filled up with any words so as to render the whole unintelligible." Each correspondent kept a similar sheet which he laid over a letter to distinguish the news from the nonsense. Very fortunately, this correspondence never met the eye of suspicious enquiry.

William had always feared that Talbot might some day wish to participate in the Forgeries, and for that reason attempted to conceal from his friend his intention of writing *Vortigern*. But the news soon spread even to Dublin, and Talbot returned to London rather indignant at having been kept from the secret, with the demand that the play be shared between them and each have the composition of a certain portion. William, fearful of exposure, was forced to agree, and promised to send a plan of some scenes to Talbot, who should write the verse and return it to him for copying into the old hand. This was the agreement; what actually happened cannot certainly be determined. William writing ten years afterwards repeatedly denies that Talbot composed any of *Vortigern*, and quotes an allegedly personal letter (dated January 6th, 1796) to prove his entire ignorance of its subject and progress. On the other hand, it is difficult to believe that anyone so persistent as Talbot would have taken neglect as calmly, and his quoted letter is wholly formal and carries but little conviction. William's vanity was such that he remained confident in the Forgeries when others already foresaw their downfall, and Talbot may willingly have surrendered his share of the credit in a work already doomed to exposure.

If Talbot was really cheated out of his part of the play, it seems highly curious that he should have come to William's rescue almost immediately afterwards, and, for the first time, stepped into the ever more tortuous tangle of deceit that surrounded the origin of the Papers. At any rate, he agreed to stand forward in support of the deception; and at the end of October, 1795, William could tell his father that Talbot, too, knew the Mysterious Gentleman, and, when he arrived in London a few days hence, would reveal the secret source of the Shakespeare manuscripts.

Samuel was in a ferment of excitement. He was staying at Brasted with Francis Webb, and left strict instructions with his daughter Jane to inform him immediately his quarry arrived in London. On November 5th Talbot was back in town, and on the following day Samuel came up and invited him to dinner. The meal proved rather a difficult one. William had probably coached his friend in his story, but in spite of his stage experience Talbot was not quick-witted, and seems to have been totally at a loss. Samuel opened the examination by showing him a letter of Mr. H.'s, making him agree that he recognised the writing, and unsuccessfully urging him to admit that the hand was that of a woman. All through dinner Samuel pressed for the reason of H.'s suspicious reticence, and the unhappy Talbot was driven to surmise "from some trifling unguarded expression," as he hastily qualified, that "one of his Ancestors was contemporary with Shakespeare in the Dramatic Profession, and that as he, H., was a man somewhat known in the world, and in the walk of high life, he did not wish such a circumstance should be made public."

Such mysterious hints served only to whet Samuel's curiosity, and Talbot further declared (probably after a kick from William) that the Gentleman had lately discovered a Deed explaining much, which he would give to William after the erasure of a tell-tale name. But in spite of his host's insistence Talbot would say no more, and gave none of the definite information that William had promised. "I pressed him much for the information I wanted," noted Samuel in his day-book, "and he said he would give it at his lodgings in Vine Street, Piccadilly, if I would go up there after I had dined, which with much reluctance I did, and found him with his brother and Mr. Cole the Apothecary, very busy packing up his trunks. After waiting some time, and pressing him very much to write me some account of the nature of the discovery of the Shake-speare Papers—he took up pen and paper and began to write, when, after writing two or three lines he desisted, and, with some eagerness, begged me to excuse him till he got into Wales, when he would write me a long and just account of the whole transaction. I expressed myself at his Conduct much hurt and dissatisfied, as having given me the trouble to come so far for no purpose, but was at length obliged to submit, and come away with much uneasiness at his Conduct—and when I reached home I then said, 'Mr. Talbot had not used me well' —and that he seemed afraid to disclose anything of the business, and this I often repeated. . . ."

Meagre as had been Talbot's disclosures they at least encouraged Samuel by suggesting a reasonable motive for the Gentleman's secrecy; and two days later he wrote to Mr. H. in a tone that was almost patronising:

The delicate predicament in which I now stand—being about to commit myself to the public in my preface to the

Shakespeare papers, will, I flatter myself, plead an apology for troubling you again in the subject of this letter. As I find I have a host of unbelievers to combat with—who are now laying in wait for my publication, and to catch at any point to serve their purpose—I will esteem it a very particular favour if you will oblige me with a few lines relative to the nature of the discovery of the papers, and that you will instruct me what you will wish me to say as to the reasons why your name should not be known. As that circumstance, you have already said, must remain a secret, I do not ask nor wish to know it, but as it is neither proper nor decent that I should throw out any hint that does not perfectly meet your idea, I think it highly necessary to address you on the subject before the work appears. After the sacred treasure you have given to my son, I fear, my Dear Sir, you will think me obtrusive in reverting to the schedule of what yet remains behind, of the pictures, books, Grant of Arms to Ireland, as mentioned in your letter about four months ago. The latter of these is a personal matter concerning my family I should be highly gratified to receive; and for the first, particularly the whole length portrait of Shakespeare of which the World has heard much talk, that being brought forth at this instant would certainly add much to the validity of the whole, and, most probably, slacken the public wish as to knowing the name of the Donor—a name that I do not think they have any right to know, nor will I ever lay any stress on knowing it in future, but as you may choose to alter your mind and freely trust it to me. Mr. Talbot a few days ago mentioned to me you had a Deed you intended to favour me with when you had erased a name in it . . . and that you have likewise a miniature pict. of the Deed, which if you will even honour me with a sight of will be the highest gratification. I know not how to apologise for this letter, but the situation I now stand in towards the Public. The Vol. is now finished printing and waits but the favour of your answer to complete. . . .

P.S. I beg to hint for your private satisfaction what passed in a private conversation some time ago with Sir Wm. Scott —who said that you need be under no fear from any Action or Suit in Chancery filed against you—for that 60 years quiet possession gives an absolute right in Law to any property whatever.

But Mr. H. did not answer in writing because, said William, he was offended to find his hand thought that of a woman.

In the meantime, Samuel had turned his attention to his son, and by his continual complaints of Talbot's conduct forced him to write a formal account of how they discovered the Papers. "I was at Chambers," scrawled William in a large hesitating hand, "when Talbot called in and showed me a Deed signed 'Shakespeare.' I was much astonished, and mentioned the pleasure my father would receive could he but see it. Talbot then said I might show it. I did for two days and at the end of that Term he gave it to me. I then pressed hard to know where it was from; after 2 or 3 days had elapsed he introduced me to the party. He was with me in the room but I took little trouble in searching. I found a second Deed and a third, and 2 or 3 loose papers. We also discovered a Deed which ascertained to the Party landed Property of which he had then no knowledge; in consequence of having found this he told us we might keep every Deed, every scrap of Paper, relating to Shakespeare. Little was discovered in town but what is above mentioned, but the rest came from the country owing to the Papers having been moved from London to the Country many years ago."

This was quite a new story, and marks William's rather tardy attempt to give his imaginings some credibility. It must have cost him considerable effort to let Talbot take the major credit for the discovery, but unfortunately Samuel had thought to question Mr. Mitchell, at whose house William first claimed to have met Mr. H., and found that the dinner his son had described in such detail had never taken place. Presumably William explained his *volte-face* on the ground of a promise to Talbot not to reveal his part in the business, and we may be sure that Samuel, who, with all his questionings, was desperately eager to be convinced, was ready enough to accept as fact the most flimsy of possibilities. This was the first mention, too, of the Deed entitling H. to landed property, and his gratitude to its discoverer offered a better explanation of his vast generosity than did a mere admiration for William's character. The believers repeatedly showed themselves willing to accept any change of story so long as it moved more towards probability.

But the complete story had to be left to Talbot, and for over a fortnight Samuel waited in vain for his promised statement from Wales. William was probably in communication with his friend, for when the long-expected letter from Carmarthen at last arrived, it had clearly been written with the utmost care and subtlety:

DEAR SIR,

If since I left London I have had a leisure moment to keep my word and write you an Account of the Papers of Shakespeare; I have not had spirits sufficiently collected, owing to hard study and hurry of Business, to give you that precise Account of them I wish you to have from my Hand. I have now the Pleasure to communicate all you will in Honor require from me, and all I can ever reveal to you and the World.

The Gentleman in whose Possession these things were found, is a Friend of mine, and by me your son Samuel was introduced to his Acquaintance. . . .

Searching from the Gent's papers, Talbot had discovered a Deed signed William Shakespeare, and finding further the words "Stratford on Avon" at once realised it must refer to the Bard himself. His first thought was to show it to his friend William, "knowing with what enthusiasm he and yourself regard the works of that Author," and although he had expected to arouse some interest, he had never anticipated the extravagant joy and excitement with which William welcomed so small a discovery. With a few artistic variations Talbot went on to repeat his friend's latest account of the valuable Deed concerning landed property, and Mr. H.'s generous gratitude for its fortunate recovery. Then, quite casually, he introduced a new and outrageous demand that William had never dared even to suggest:

Shortly after this I left London (as you may remember) on my favourite pursuit, but previous to my Departure made the following Agreement with my Friend Sam; that if he fortunately should discover any paper of Shakespeare's, from the Publication or use of which any pecuniary advantage might accrue—such profit should be equally divided between us. . . . whilst I was in Dublin, I heard to my great Joy and Astonishment that Sam had discovered amongst the Lumber the Play of Vortigern and Rowena, the manuscript of Lear, etc. I was impatient to hear every particular, and principally for that Purpose made my late Visit to London. I found H. (what I always thought him) a man of strict honor, and willing to abide by the Promise he made, in consequence of our finding the Deed by which he benefited so much. He left us to adjust the Division of the Profits, and the following Resolution made between Sam and myself met with his Compliance; that in consequence of Samuel's Diligence and my Negligence in searching for the valuable articles, and some other agreements between ourselves (which are immaterial to mention) that had been made before my Departure from London; I should *not* receive, as we had agreed, an equal share, but that Sam should receive two-thirds of the Profits arising from the performing and publishing the Play of Vortigern and Rowena, and I only one.

However slow Talbot might be in emergency, as a writer of difficult letters he was above reproach. First, the shocking but casual assumption of a fifty per cent. division with no mention of Mr. Ireland; then an enumeration of the possible sources of profit, and a statement in advance of Mr. H.'s concurrence with what the pair had agreed; then an emphatic disavowal of the first outrageous claim; and finally a quite clear and definite agreement as displeasing to Samuel as any that could reasonably be imagined. The last paragraph, with its apparent utter withdrawal and disclaimer down to the harmless insignificance of the final "one," might serve as a perfect model for the technique of breaking things gently. This division of profits was probably Talbot's price for supporting the crumbling foundation of William's deceit and, just possibly, for abandoning his share in the composition of *Vortigern*. He seems hardly the man to have made either concession for nothing.

Having given the pill, Talbot hastened to sweeten it with a hint of the Gent's identity:

I will now explain the Reason of H.'s secrecy. On account of your Desire to give to the World some Explanation of the Business, and your telling me that such explanation was necessary, I renewed my Entreaties to him to suffer us to discover his Name, Place of Abode, and some circumstances of the Discovery of the Papers, but in vain. I proceeded to prove as well as I could the Folly of its Concealment, when he produced a Deed of Gift which he had himself found in the closet just before my Departure from London in January last; but which I had never seen before. By this Deed William Shakespeare assigned to John ——, who it seems, was really an ancestor of our friend H, every article contained in an upper room, in consequence of their having passed together many Evenings in mild Discourse, and in smoaking their Pipes together in that very Apartment. The Articles, as Furniture, Cups, Miniature Picture, and many other things, are specified in the Deed, but excepting the Miniature (which has lately been found among the Lumber, and which is a Likeness of Shakespeare himself), very few of them remain in H's hands, and the rest unfortunately cannot be traced. It is supposed that many valuable papers have been lost or destroyed, as the whole Lumber is never remembered as being at all valued, or guarded from the destructive hands of the lowest Domestics. . . . H. promised me that the Deed of Gift above mentioned should be sent you, first erasing or cutting out the name of the grantee. At my last Visit to my friend H. with Sam, he again enjoined us never to make his Name known to anyone, declaring if we did he would immediately revoke his Promise, and claim the whole again as his own Property. . . .

Samuel was very annoyed. He neither replied to Talbot's letter nor admitted his claim for the money, and brusquely informed his son that he would refuse to accept the promised Deed if any name was erased. William realised he had presumed too far, and, without further quibbling, produced a Deed of Trust from Shakespeare to his friend John Heming:

I William Shakspeare being of Stratforde on Avon but now living in Londonn doe make and orderr this as and for mye Deede of gifte HAVING founde muche wickedness amongste those of the lawe and not liking to leave matterrs at theyre wills I have herein named a trusty and tried friende who shall afterr mye dethe execute withe care myne orderrs herein given. . . . Firste untoe mye deare Wife I doe orderr as folowithe thatt she bee payde withinne oune monthe afterre mye dethe the somme of oune hondrythe and fowre score Pounds fromme the moneys whyche be nowe laynge onn Accompte of the Globe Theatre inn the hands of Master John Hemynge ALSOE I doe give herr mye suyte of greye Vellvett edged withe Silverr tog^r withe mye lyttelle Cedarr Trunke in wyche there bee three Ryngs oune lyttell payntyng of myselfe in a silverr Case & sevenn leterrs wrottenn to her before oure Marryage these I doe beg herr toe keepe safe if everr she dydd love me— Toe mye deare Daughterr who hathe alwaye demeaned herrselfe well I doe give . . . mye suyte of blacke silke & the Rynge whyche I doe alwaye weare givenne toe mee bye hys Grace of Southampton thys I doe beg herr as she dothe love mee neverr toe parte fromm. . . .

Shakespeare went on to distribute gifts of money and clothes to his friends and fellow-actors, and shared out of the manuscripts of all the plays in "the Oakenn Cheste att oure Globe Theatre," including his "chose Interrlude neverr yette Impryntedd and wrottenn for and bye desyre of oure late gracyosse and belovedd Quene Elizabethe called ye Virginn Quene." But the Deed charged Heming with more than a mere distribution, and revealed a new element in Shakespeare's story that might at last explain the secrecy of Mr. H.

I furtherr orderr hym [Hemynge] toe brynge upp that Chylde of whom wee have spokenn butt who muste nott be named here & to doe same I desyre hum toe place owte s^d. Moneye in ye beste waye he cann doe tylle s^d. Childe shall be of Age toe receyve s^d. Moneye & withe whatte shall comm uppon s^d. Moneye soe toe Instructe hym as aforesayde. . . . I allsoe give toe s^d. Chylde y^e. eyghte Playes thatt bee stylle inne s^d. Cheste as allso mye otherr Playe neverr yett Imprynted called Kynge Vorrtygerne . . . and shoulde I chaunce write more as bye Gods helpe & grace I hope toe doe I herebye give ye Profytts of evry Kynde comynge fromm anye suche newe playes orr otherr Wrytyngs unntoe s^d. Chylde & hys heires forr everre trustynge toe mye freynde John Hemynges honorr and allso onn hys promys of beynge clouse of speeche inn thys laste Matterr. . . .

Presumably Heming deserted his trust and absconded with the money and *King Vortigern*. Dare we guess that Shakespeare's other great friend adopted the child, made him his heir, and gave him the name of "Ireland"?

By the end of 1795 Samuel's doubts were resolved once and for all. He had long been desirous of winning Royal patronage for his discoveries, and his joy must have been extreme at receiving a letter from Carlton House summoning him to an audience with the Prince of Wales. At 12.30 on the morning of the 28th of December, Mr. Jerningham arrived as his escort, and after proudly showing the manuscripts to his somewhat unresponsive visitor, Samuel sent for a coach to drive them to the Presence. As they were leaving, word came from Albany Wallis, Samuel's friend and neighbour in Norfolk Street, demanding an immediate interview and refusing to be stayed. "Mr. Wallis, when he entered the middle room, said (putting his hand towards his pocket) 'I have here something to show you that will do your business for you, and knock up your Shakespeare papers,'—this was said in the presence of Mr. Jerningham, who was standing by the fire."

Samuel was shocked beyond measure, and ignoring Mr. Jerningham's eye on the clock, called him and Wallis into his study, and insisted on knowing the worst. The truth was simple and entirely damning. Albany Wallis, in the course of his continual researches, had discovered the original Conveyance of the house that Shakespeare had bought in Blackfriars. Amongst the Trustees signing the Deed was a Jno. Heminge, obviously the Poet's friend and fellow-actor. But the signature was wholly and completely different from that on the Heming Receipt, one of the earliest discovered of the Shakespeare Papers. To Albany Wallis' open triumph and Mr. Jerningham's tactful silence, Samuel could make no answer; there was simply nothing to say. The audience at Carlton House lasted over two hours and, according to the Press, the Prince of Wales "was pleased to bestow very particular attention on [the Papers], and to express his perfect conviction of their undoubted authenticity." Samuel makes no comment on the interview; he probably appreciated very little of it.

At two o'clock William strolled in from the office and learned the dreadful news. He hurried immediately to see Wallis, hopelessly praying that the genuine hand might bear at least some faint resemblance to that of his own invention. One glance showed him the vanity of such a hope; the signature that Wallis held out and triumphantly waved in his face was wholly dissimilar to that of the forged receipt. He ran home a few minutes later wildly searching for ways of escape, "and, as the family said, seemed very much agitated, and the sweat seemed to drop from his brow. He said he would go to the Gent. and mention the circumstance." William hurried from the house to his office at New Inn.

Half an hour later he returned to Wallis and showed him four receipts signed John Heming, tied in a bundle with about twenty others. Wallis and a friend compared the new signatures with the original in their possession and found with astonishment that they bore a close resemblance to it and were clearly by the same hand. Urged to explain the source of these fresh discoveries, William "said that when he entered the Gentleman's room and told him the agitation of his mind on the occasion, the Gentleman said: 'Young man—don't be disconcerted, we'll see if we can't relieve you'—then turning to his Guest, he searched among a large parcel of old papers and gave the parcel before alluded to."

Samuel returned from Carlton House to find the papers re-established and the scoffing Wallis converted to whole-hearted acceptance. There could be no further doubt that the manuscripts were authentic.

The forgery of the receipts was the most remarkable of all William's exploits. He had obtained no more than a glimpse of the genuine signature, without any opportunity to trace or even to study it. All the witnesses are agreed that he returned to the house in under half an hour, so that, allowing for the journey to and from his office, he had about twenty minutes in which to forge at least four papers and possibly many others. Albany Wallis was not such an easy dupe as Samuel or Webb; he was a genuine scholar of a cynical turn of mind, and his acceptance of the fresh signatures was certainly not dictated by a blind wish to believe, but could only have arisen from a real conviction of their genuineness. William himself was not quite satisfied with his work, and took back the receipts to write out again at his leisure. When the first excitement had died down he was closely questioned to explain the dissimilarity between his first receipt and the genuine signature. He said that the Gent. had revealed the existence of *two* John Hemings, both connected with the Theatre and both acquainted with Shakespeare. The Poet's great friend, who had signed Wallis' Deed, was the *tall* John Heming of the Globe, but there had also been a *short* John Heming of the Curtain Theatre, who had written the first receipt.

Coolly regarded, the story was highly improbable, and the coincidence of the second discovery seemed as strange as it was fortunate. But nothing could alter the fact that the signatures had been found under conditions that seemed absolutely to preclude any possibility of forgery. Samuel's own doubts were set quite at rest, and some even of the Papers' enemies were visibly shaken in their unbelief. The accident that should have brought William's downfall had merely increased his prestige. He had every excuse for thinking himself a genius.

Chapter Nine

NEGOTIATIONS FOR *"VORTIGERN"*

As soon as Samuel had announced that the Papers included an unknown full-length play, it was universally realised that the strongest literary and financial reasons demanded its early presentation on the public stage; and the two great Managers approached Mr. Ireland to treat for the rights of production. The first on the scene was Richard Brinsley Sheridan, part owner of Drury Lane Theatre, and then at the height of his reputation. Sheridan's career had been a romantic and splendid one. While still a youth he eloped to France with Elizabeth Linley, daughter of the composer, fought two sword duels on her behalf, and won some repute as a serious actor. But his fame really began when, in partnership with his father-in-law, he purchased the Drury Lane Theatre and made it an even greater success than it had been in the days of Garrick; taking, it was said, a personal profit of £10,000 a year. As playwright and politician he was equally distinguished, and won such parliamentary popularity that, on the news that his theatre was in flames, the House offered to adjourn in sympathy for their member's misfortune. Most of his contemporaries praise Sheridan's charm and courtesy, though Samuel was to find these qualities rather over-rated.

As a friend of Thomas Linley, Samuel had a personal connection with the Theatre, and he probably decided as soon as the play was discovered, that Drury Lane should have the honour of producing *Vortigern*. Towards the end of March, 1795, Sheridan called at Norfolk Street to read part of the manuscript, and seems to have come to a verbal agreement for its presentation. At any rate, when Thomas Harris of Covent Garden Theatre called to inspect the papers the following week, Samuel rejected his advances, although, according to William, he offered a blank contract of production without even reading the play. It seems a great pity that Samuel refused his offer, for Harris was an excellent showman and would certainly have presented *Vortigern* with pomp and publicity. To the end of his life, William never ceased to regret his father's misplaced loyalty to his friends at Drury Lane.

When Sheridan read the whole of *Vortigern* he began to regret his first acceptance. It was not that he doubted the authenticity of the manuscript; he simply considered the new Shakespeare an inferior dramatist and not really fit for the stage of so great a theatre. The famous author of *The School for Scandal* had little use for the Bard; "however high Shakespeare might stand in the estimation of the public in general, he did not for his part regard him as a poet in that exalted light, although he allowed the brilliancy of his ideas and the penetration of his mind." Even this sober estimate was a little disappointed by the new discovery, and after reading several pages of *Vortigern* Sheridan was driven to remark:

"This is rather strange; for though you are acquainted with my opinion as to Shakespeare, yet, be it as it may, he certainly always wrote poetry."

After reading a few pages further, he again paused to make a pronouncement:

"There are certainly some bold ideas, but they are crude and undigested. It is very odd: one would be led to think that Shakespeare must have been very young when he wrote the play. As to the doubting whether it really be his or not, who can possibly look at the papers and not believe them ancient?"

As the weeks passed Sheridan became increasingly unwilling to commit his acceptance to writing. Fruitless discussions dragged from March into April, and from April till the end of May, but still there was no agreement as to the terms of production. Though neither party would admit it, both feared for the run of the piece, and wanted to take their profit on the certain receipts of a sensational opening week. Samuel demanded a large advance and a considerable share in the first few performances, while the Management wished to make no payment down but merely to pay a nightly percentage over the whole run. At last it became clear that no arrangement could be reached without mediation, and both sides resolved to leave the decision to the judgment of Albany Wallis.

The first shot came from Sheridan:

> The Proprietors of the Drury Lane Theatre wish to deal in the most liberal manner with Mr. Ireland, and are ready to leave to Mr. Wallis's arbitration the terms on which the play of *Vortigern* should be produced. They conceive that the fairest and the most honourable grounds to proceed on would be to assign to Mr. Ireland a proportion of the first forty nights' receipts. The compensation will then be contingent on the success, and if that answers present expectation it will be a most considerable sum.

This did not in the least appeal to Samuel, and on the following day he made his counter-demand, asking £500 down and six clear nights' receipts (instead of the three nights usually allowed to the authors of new plays), three of these nights to be in the first ten performances. Sheridan replied with the suggestion of £200 down and six nights' takings, less a nightly establishment charge of £220; an offer that Samuel indignantly rejected, countering with a proposal for an advance of £250 and the surplus over £220 for twenty nights.

Samuel could not understand such meanness on so great an occasion, and pathetically jots down in his note-book:

> "Speak to Sheridan abt.
> Swift's MSS
> Pope's and Addison's."

But Sheridan seemed to have no conception of the respect due to Shakespeare, and was ready to haggle over a trifling percentage when he was offered the chance of revealing the Bard's new glory. By July he was breaking his appointments, and Samuel began to have doubts of his integrity, wondering unhappily how to assure a proper assessment and delivery of the nightly profits. He continually tried to arrange a meeting, and waited in vain at home or at the Drury Lane only to be told that the Manager was away, or engaged on very particular business. "Such frequent disappointments," wrote Samuel after one of these fruitless vigils, "render it necessary now to be informed what are really your intentions with regard to signing the agreement for the play, as I am waiting in Town on that matter alone, and my son likewise is prevented from going into the Country on a very material business both to himself and to me. I therefore request the favor of an immediate answer, as it will admit of no longer delay." But the immediate answer was not forthcoming, and it was not until September 9th, 1795, that Albany Wallis forced Sheridan actually to sign an Agreement. "WHEREAS the said Samuel Ireland is possessed of a certain Ancient Manuscript play, called or intitled Vortigern, and signed and supposed to be written by William Shakespeare, AND WHEREAS the said Richard Brinsley Sheridan and Thomas Linley have agreed with the said Samuel Ireland . . . ", began the lawyers cautiously, and proceeded to give Albany Wallis' idea of a reasonable compromise. Samuel was to receive £250 down and half the nightly takings in excess of £350, while Sheridan for his part guaranteed a minimum run of forty nights, provided the takings never fell below an average of £220 a performance. It was further agreed that the play should be produced before December 15th.

These were very stiff terms. It was true that the theatre had taken £648 on the opening night after its rebuilding, and that three nights of *The School for Scandal* had brought Sheridan nearly £650 after all deductions had been made. But these were exceptional occasions; the average takings over a run of forty nights were only £313 a performance, and *Vortigern* would have to achieve quite an exceptional success to bring its possessor more than the mere advance. At the time the contract was drawn up Samuel's apprehensions about the genuineness of the manuscripts were at their height, and this probably made him more amenable to the Management's demands than would otherwise have been the case. But even had he been convinced in his own mind, there was really no other alternative to acceptance of Sheridan's terms, however bad they might be. The long delay over negotiations had not been accidental, but had the definite purpose of cutting off Samuel from his only other market. Eager as was the Covent Garden to produce *Vortigern*, it would never accept a play after months of submission to its greatest rival. By September Samuel realised that he must accept the Drury Lane terms or have no production at all.

If Mr. Ireland imagined that his troubles with the theatre were over he was very much mistaken, for Sheridan continued, as if out of malice, the procrastination he had first pursued for policy. There was even delay in paying the agreed advance, and early in October we find him still promising that the money would shortly be ready, and still apologising for breaking his appointments. The advance was finally paid, but Sheridan would do nothing else to implement the agreement, and quite ignored Samuel's requests for an interview. "I waited on Tuesday more than two hours after your appointment at the theatre—to what purpose I need not say," wrote Samuel indignantly, "I likewise called on Greenwood [the stage carpenter] the next morning expecting to see some progress made in his design for Vortigern—and then to my great surprise I learned that he had had an order from some person about the theatre to lay aside the Designs and begin the scenery for a *pantomime*. This Conduct is so different from that which your Conversation on the subject seemed to imply, that I am really at a loss to know what is intended, and shall be happy to have a line from you on the subject. . . ." But there was no reply.

From early in April Sheridan seems to have regretted his decision to produce *Vortigern*, and attempted in every way to go back on his first undertaking. Now, with the contract signed and the realisation that the increasing strength of the opposition made the success of the venture ever more dubious, he resolved to cut expenses to the minimum, and, in spite of his verbal promise to produce the play on a magnificent scale (it was only on this understanding that Samuel had agreed to the enormous deduction of £350 for expenses), determined to make do with the old costumes and touched up scenery of previous historical tragedies. His immediate object was to obtain the manuscript of *Vortigern* which Samuel still kept for copying into modern English, and he instructed Kemble, his actor-manager, to write and demand its immediate delivery.

Samuel's suspicions were now fully aroused, and he replied strongly:

"It is now more than three months since you gave order to Mr. Greenwood, while I was present, to proceed with the scenery for Vortigern, and I am much surprised after so long a time has elapsed, to find no attention has been paid to that order, or that it has given place to subsequent directions. I am the more surprised to have received a pressing letter from Mr. Kemble requesting that the MS. might be immediately forwarded to him. This urgency I do not apprehend can be necessary—unless it is intended to substitute old Scenery for the new ones which you have always promised should be prepared. I therefore beg the favour of a line from you to know what is really your intention as to the scenery, as in the course of a week I shall be ready to fulfil my promise to deliver the MS."

Sheridan answered soothingly, and arranged a meeting between Samuel and Kemble for November 17th, when the delay in the scenery should be fully explained and the outstanding disagreements settled. The appointment, as usual, was broken, and Samuel at last decided on counter-measures:

Agreeable to your appointment I was with my Son at the Theatre before 2 o'clock this day, when to my great surprise I found Mr. Kemble had left the house, although I had previously informed him of your appointment at that hour.

As I find from all quarters that Mr. Kemble is a luke-warm friend to the play—I refer myself to *you* to know *your design* as to the *scenery*, which certainly may be forwarded by Mr. Greenwood without the manuscript, which I repeat to you is quite ready.

But my friends have all but one opinion with myself, *that as you have given orders* for new scenery three months ago, and nothing yet done, that I am strictly justified in keeping back the MS. My situation with regard to the piece is not that of a mere author. I have a great stake at risk, and much will depend on your exertions with regard to the Play. . . . I beg the favour of you to give me an immediate answer by letter, that I may understand more fully your intentions, and that I may not lose so much time in attending appointments that seem made only for the purpose of breaking them.

It is difficult to understand the motive for Sheridan's behaviour. Samuel observes in a letter that "Mr. Sheridan has not used us well, but what can be expected of a man who never seriously attends to anything"; but his attitude certainly cannot be explained merely as the absent-minded casualness of a busy dilettante. Sheer lazy inefficiency was as little in Sheridan's character as was a moral cowardice that would have compelled him to implement legally a verbal agreement he afterwards came to regret. It seems probable that Thomas Linley, Samuel's old friend, was the prime mover behind the acceptance of *Vortigern*; and that Sheridan, unable openly to oppose his partner's wishes, attempted to drive Samuel into breaking the agreement himself and withdrawing the play from presentation. If this was the case Samuel's position was made still more unfavourable by Linley's sudden death on November 19th; and although Sheridan had gone too far actually to default on the contract, the last restraints on his hostility vanished, and he openly flouted promises, obligations and ordinary courtesy.

The Management's only reply to their victim's latest letter was to demand the immediate delivery of the manuscript or the return of the advance payment. Samuel was now quite convinced that they intended to use "old or vamped scenery," and for the first time hinted at legal action, pointing out that less than a month remained to the contracted date of production. Sheridan saw he had tried his dupe too hard, and sent him a copy of an order to Greenwood instructing the immediate commencement of work on the scenery for *Vortigern*. But Greenwood was strangely slow, and to Samuel's demand for haste could only reply:

> SIR,
> I have not seen Mr. Sheridan since he was with you att the Theatre; on Saturday Mr. Grub was with me. I propose'd away to him to gett itt done agreeable to your Desire. I expect the Business to be settled today as Mr. Grub din'd with Mr. S. on Saturday and promised to see this morning.
> Your humbl ser^t
> THOS. GREENWOOD.

Samuel hurried round to the carpenter's shop to investigate, and furiously reminded Greenwood of Sheridan's written instructions. But the carpenter only said that "he could not, consistently with the order from the house, pay any attention." At last Samuel clearly realised that Sheridan and Kemble were among his most dangerous enemies, and with a tardy but desperate firmness he flatly refused to give up the manuscript until he saw with his own eyes that work on the scenery had actually been commenced. Sheridan thought the time had come for more tactful methods, and we find young Linley, the son of Samuel's old friend, apologising for the Management's apparent discourtesy, and promising to see that something was done to hasten forward the production. "My mother desires me to say," he continued, "that she most particularly wishes you to send the play to Mr. Kemble—she says she has reasons for it which she will explain to you when she sees you." At first glance this looks a particularly mean attempt to trick Samuel by an appeal to an old friendship, and unfortunately I can find no further reference to Mrs. Linley's secret reasons. It is possible, however, that she was in Sheridan's confidence and really advised Samuel for the best, in the knowledge that a tardy and tawdry presentation was better than none at all. But Samuel was not to be moved, and again threatened legal action to uphold the terms of the contract.

At the end of December the situation suddenly changed. On the 27th Kemble wrote to Mr. Ireland making no mention of the delay or the scenery, but demanding the immediate delivery of the manuscript, with a bland reproof for the tardiness of its preparation. Samuel sent the play by return with a pathetic request to his enemy to "see justice done." He had no more fight left in him, for at last he had published *Miscellaneous Papers under the Hand and Seal of William Shakespeare*, and must face the world on a definite issue. The first few days of the publication had shown him with dreadful clarity that he must hasten the production of *Vortigern* regardless of contracts, understandings or personal pride.

The winter months of 1795 had not been wholly without their compensations. On November 18th Samuel and his son were summoned to St. James's Palace to show the manuscript to the Duke of Clarence, and were graciously received by the purple prince himself, Mrs. Jordan, the actress, his mistress, and an unnamed clergyman. The audience was probably given at the instance of Mrs. Jordan, who was to take one of the leading parts in *Vortigern*, and the Duke loudly encouraged the gratified Samuel by remarking that he highly approved of his decision to withhold the play until the scenery was begun, and warning him to "beware the conduct of the Manager, who was one of the greatest vagabonds on the face of the earth and his deputy the greatest Jesuit." Not content merely with verbal encouragement His Royal Highness ordered seven copies of the forthcoming *Miscellaneous Papers*, five for himself and two for his son Edward.

William was immensely attracted by Mrs. Jordan. As an actress she was not comparable to Mrs. Siddons, and the crustier critics agreed with Samuel's friend the Hon. John Byng, that "Mrs. Jordan may jump about in romps and such like, but knows nothing of Juliets, Rosalinds, and Imogens. It is not age but skill." But most of her contemporaries agree with Hazlitt, who called her "the child of nature whose voice is a cordial to the heart . . . who talked far above singing," and with Reynolds, who said "she ran upon the stage as on a playground." Like almost all who met and knew her however slightly, William remained her admirer as long as he lived. For her part, she seems to have taken a fancy to the shy, clever, good-looking young man who had discovered the manuscripts; and, almost alone of the actors who performed in it, did everything in her power to make *Vortigern* a success.

At the beginning of December, William announced the

discovery of *another* play, entitled *Henry II*. According to his own account, he wrote it in ten weeks and presented it to his father in modern handwriting immediately it was completed, declaring that the Gentleman had refused to allow the play to be removed until he had made a complete copy. *Henry II*, which dealt with the downfall of a rather Wolsey-esque Becket, is far superior to *Vortigern* both technically and poetically, and had it preceded the latter would probably have won a far greater success. As it was, the increasing tumult around the earlier papers distracted attention from this latest treasure, and it was not until after the production of its predecessor that it came into public notice.

Just before Christmas Samuel fulfilled his promise of the early spring, and published *Miscellaneous Papers and Legal Instruments under the Hand and Seal of William Shakespeare . . . from the original manuscripts in the possession of Samuel Ireland*. Beneath this imposing title was the motto:

> *"Quod optanti Divum promittere nemo*
> *Auderet volvenda Dies en attulit ultro."*

while the whole was dedicated to the

Ingenuous, Intelligent, and Disinterested,
Whose Candour, Conviction, and Support
Have given the Sanction
To the Publication of
THESE PAPERS.

The volume was produced in large folio, with coloured reproductions of the drawings and of Willy's lock of hair, and facsimiles of all the papers save *Lear* and *Hamlet*.

In his Preface, Samuel abjured all doubts and allowed no

shadow of caution to mar the glory of the precious manuscript. "Throughout this period," he boasted, "there has not been an ingenuous character, or disinterested individual, in the circle of Literature, to whose critical eye he has not been earnest that the whole should be subjected. He has courted, he has even challenged, the critical judgment of those who are best skilled in the Poetry and Phraseology of the time in which Shakespeare lived; as well as those whose profession or course of study has made them conversant with ancient Deeds, writings, seals and autographs. Wide and extensive as this range may appear, and it includes the Scholar, the Man of Taste, the Antiquarian and the Herald, his enquiries have not rested in the closet of the Speculatist; he has been equally anxious that the whole should be submitted to the practical experience of the Mechanic, and be pronounced upon by the paper-maker, etc., as well as the Author. He has ever been desirous of placing them in any view and under any light that could be thrown upon them; and he has, in consequence, the satisfaction of announcing to the Public that . . . they had unanimously testified in favour of their authenticity; and declared that where there was such a mass of evidence internal and external, it was impossible, amidst such various sources of detection, for the art of imitation to have hazarded so much without betraying itself; and, consequently, that *these Papers can be no other than the production of Shakespeare himself.*"

He proceeds to recount, in very little detail, the story of the mysterious Gentleman, but hastens to stress the obvious truth that the identity of the donor or the source of his generosity are quite beside the point; if the critic cannot judge the papers by themselves, then "his lucubrations are idle and useless."

Who would dare counterfeit Shakespeare? "So superior and transcendant is the Genius of Shakespeare, that scarce any attempts to rival or imitate him, and those too contemptible to notice, have ever been made. With a wit so pregnant, and an imagination so unbounded, such an intuitive knowledge of the workings of the human heart, so simple and so sublime, it seemed, that the seal of heaven had been stamped upon the production of his mind." But besides the obvious genius of the manuscripts there was another reason for unquestioning acceptance; the newly discovered papers not only added to our literary heritage, but enhanced the reputation of the poet himself by showing a character as noble as his talents were extraordinary. "The [manuscripts] exhibit him in a new character—unite with the Bard, the Critic and the Moralist, and display an acute and penetrating judgment, with a disposition amiable and gentle as his Genius was transcendant. Such a view of our immortal Poet must prove highly acceptable to every sincere admirer."

Samuel had put a bolder face on it than many even of his own supporters would have approved. Unfortunately, the Ingenuous and Intelligent were now by no means disinterested.

Chapter Ten

THE CONTROVERSY

The publication of *Miscellaneous Papers* turned private discussion into popular controversy. For over a year the Papers had remained in Samuel's sole possession with all the sacrosanct secrecy of private property; and although in theory they were open to inspection by any friend of a Subscriber, in practice the treasures could be examined only by Samuel's guests, with all the inhibition of criticism such a relation implied. Now the discoveries were fully exposed to the world; "criticism," as the *True Briton* justly observed, "has here a feast upon which it may gorge itself." The vultures did not delay long.

The first on the scene was James Boaden, editor of the *Oracle*. Boaden had originally been amongst the staunchest of the believers, and the paper he edited was responsible for many of the more ridiculous encomiums on the precious relics. After a few months, however, his enthusiasm began noticeably to cool, probably under the influence of his friend George Steevens, the Shakespearian critic; and, without showing open hostility, he ceased to see Samuel or to write in praise of his Discoveries. After a period of neutrality the *Oracle* began to move towards the opposition, and published "extracts" from the promised *Vortigern*, in which Boaden showed what he thought was skill as a Shakespearian versifier, and treated his readers to extensive passages of empty but harmless rhetoric:

> *Whatte if I flye and hidde the Britain Bandes*
> *Howe Vortimer! a rebell to thye kinge!*
> *Thatte kinge a father too! O wretched state*

O bosom tortured betweene love and dutye
Maye notte hostilitie at times be mercye,
As the wise lucke from bodilye gangerene
Preserves the noble parts by amputacioun? . . .

This sort of thing was not scurrilous, it was not even openly parody, but its effect was certainly slanderous. The antique spelling, the implied claim that the verse was as good as that in Samuel's manuscript, were hostile in effect if not entirely in intention, while the disparagement gained an additional force by appearing in a quarter that had previously been strong in adherence to the Discoveries.

Boaden was not a subscriber to the published manuscripts, and on the eve of publication he called at Norfolk Street to beg the loan of a copy. Samuel was not at home, and Mrs. Freeman, apparently unsure of the position, promised to send a volume directly a new supply came from the binders. Boaden thereupon left a note of his request, and when Samuel returned, he learned that "the proprietors of the *Oracle* present their compliments to Mr. Ireland. They use the freedom to request the loan of his Shakespeare, and will exert every means to keep the work in the public eye."

Mr. Ireland rightly regarded this letter as a piece of deliberate insolence, and, very mistakenly, replied in appropriate terms. "Mr. Ireland feels himself highly flattered by the *good intentions of the proprietors of the Oracle* in wishing to lay before the public any part of his volume from the Shakespeare MSS, but as he does not feel it necessary to call in any auxiliary support in aid of the ground on which he stands—that of Truth—he begs to decline lending the work alluded to in their note."

This justifiable sharpness had very serious consequences.

The *Oracle* immediately dropped even the pretence of friendship, and met Samuel's challenge with a libellous address from Maister William Shakespeare in the Shades to Samuel Ireland Esq.:

> CONUNDRUMS! LOVE LETTERS! PROFESSIONS de foi
> *And straggling* INDENTURES *in form* de la loi
> *A copy corrected of Britain's old* LEAR
> (*Where with pleasure I see nothing ribald appear*).
> *And to these many sports of the sons of the* STAGE
> *Add the favourite works in retirement of* AGE
> *On which my weak brain you affirm set more store*
> *Than all it had ever engendered before.*

This casual lampoon was merely a stop-gap; and before the news of the quarrel was widely known Boaden borrowed a volume of *Miscellaneous Papers* from one of the Believers, and proceeded to serialise the Manuscripts with an insulting and damaging commentary. Others of the Press were not slow to follow his example.

The open revelation of Boaden's enmity showed Samuel Ireland the full danger of his position. The best defence was to anticipate his opponents, and a few days later he wrote to his friend Francis Webb suggesting, or rather commanding, the immediate composition of a pamphlet in support of the Manuscripts. Webb was not very happy about the proposal. He still believed in the genuineness of the discoveries, but realised more clearly than did Samuel the increasing difficulty of their situation, and awaited with equal dread Malone's inevitable onslaught and the promised presentation of *Vortigern*. He vainly suggested Dr. Parr as a suitable substitute for the doubtful honour of opening the defence, but Samuel remained insistent, and, early in January, Webb forwarded the original draft of an essay, whose warm and direct affirmations won Samuel's whole-hearted approval. In the meantime, however, the enemy had got in first.

At the beginning of February, 1796, James Boaden published *A Letter to George Steevens Esq. Containing a Critical Examination of the Shakespeare Manuscripts,* in which he attacked the Discoveries with a bitterness only exceeded by the warmth of his early acceptance. He was probably too well acquainted with Samuel to believe him guilty of the forgeries and, almost alone of the opposition, suspected William of the major part in the deception. In the manuscript of *Lear* he was fortunate enough to discover "hélas" for "alas," and observes that "by this curious mode of writing the interjection, one might be tempted to believe that Shakespeare had received a French education at the College of St. Omers," while elsewhere he delicately but not too distantly hints at William's familiarity with ancient documents and Talbot's gift of dramatic imitation.

Apart from general invective he had very little to say. He makes the good point that Elizabeth's letter to Shakespeare commanding him to bring his best players for the entertainment of herself and Leicester, must have been written before that nobleman's death in 1588, whereas in 1592 we find Shakespeare describing *Venus and Adonis* as the first heir of his invention; a curious fact if four years earlier he was already sufficiently famous to attract the rare personal interest of the Queen herself. Besides a few telling but indecisive points of this kind, and a number of jeering observations on the versification of the Papers, Boaden was singularly ineffective. Spite against Samuel and a rather parasitical regard for George Steevens supplied the place of any ardent conviction of the fraudulence of the Discoveries.

In his heart of hearts Boaden thought very little of Shakespeare, and may have regarded some of William's emendations as definite improvements upon the original. Even in this professed defence of the Poet's reputation, he remarks reprovingly that "in his efforts after the lofty and sublime he is frequently turgid and diffuse; his meaning is often buried under the pomp of his expression and a very feeble thought lies like a titled idiot entombed in marble, and surrounded by the graces of too lavish art"; and, with shameless sophistry, proceeds to argue that the very restraint and simplicity of the Manuscripts prove that they must have been fabricated. Boaden was capable of detecting unmetrical verse, and pillories unmercifully such enormities as:

> *Thatte these heartte teares thatte breake fromme*
> *Mee perforce shoud make worse blasts ande Foggs*
> *Onne the unnetennederre woundynges of a Fatherres*
> *Usse playe thys parte agayne . . .*

Yet if the lines scanned, his taste was easily satisfied, and the worst he can find to say against the verses to Anna is that they are "worthy of no other notice than that they are metrically smooth."

In everything but the accident of his personal motives James Boaden was a perfect type of the Believer, and poured from his own pen the same sort of poetry he had previously admired in the Forgeries. In 1790 he presented *Fontainville Forest* at Covent Garden Theatre, and entertained its approving patrons to an evening of such grand versification as:

Despair has laid his callous hand upon me
And fitted me for deeds from which I once
Had shrunk with horror—I have no resource
But robbery—the degradation! What!
To nourish guilty life turn common stabber!
Lurk in a hedge, and like an adder sting
The unguarded passenger! Well, and what then? . . .

The drama was received with much applause and went through
several printed editions. Boaden apparently regarded the
Manuscripts as a personal poetic challenge, for at the end of his
pamphlet he reprints the whole of the Shakespearian imitations
that had lumbered on heavy feet through the pages of the
Oracle. Is it possible that his opposition to the Papers was
partly the outcome of professional jealousy?

A few days after the appearance of *A Letter to George Steevens*,
Webb, under the happy disguise of "Philalethes," published
Shakespeare's Manuscripts Examined. Having written his defence
before the appearance of the first attack, he had very little to
say, and wisely refrained from the two-edged tactic of making
criticisms only in order to refute them. His pamphlet contents
itself with repeating in print the ecstatic remarks heard so often
in Samuel's study; his only original arguments are the doubtful
point that the Papers combine to confirm each other, and the
still more dubious plea that the very errors of the Manuscripts
proved their authenticity, since a forger would certainly have
taken greater trouble. "I am not only fully satisfied of their
authenticity," cries Philalethes, "but also . . . I am as fully
satisfied and believe, that no human wisdom, cunning, art or
deceit if they could be united are equal to the task of such an
imposition." Again, forgers are notoriously cautious and

sensible people who take as few risks as is humanly possible, so what man in his senses, save Shakespeare himself, would have ventured to compose most of the precious papers?

Would it [deception] not probably have contented itself with less minute and circumstantial evidence than that of a lock of the Poet's own hair, plaited too with the hands of the Bard in braid of love, and presented to the obscure damsel with a letter and copy of verses such as that which a simple swain, as he then was, would have transmitted to his fair? O! no—Nature and Nature alone produces documents like these. They are marked with the authentic seal of her artless simplicity. These are fine touches which imposture can never imitate. It knows full well it is not equal to the task, and therefore never attempts it. . . . Imposture in general keeps within bounds of probability.

Poor Webb had done his best.

Webb's early suggestion that Dr. Parr should be asked to defend the discoveries he had so warmly supported, appealed to Samuel, and when it was widely reported that both Steevens and Malone were preparing to launch really learned attacks on the Papers, he wrote to the Doctor and diffidently sought his assistance:

Malone's pamphlet is to appear in about a week, and one from the pen of Steevens about the same time or before if possible, as they are running a race to see who has the first hit. . . . Their opposition is, I hear, to be principally supported by an attempt to prove that the orthography of Shakespeare's MS. is not that of the period in which he lived. . . .

If on the further investigation of these treasures you should still be convinced of their authenticity, I need not say that the aid of your pen on so great an occasion and, as I hope, in the cause of truth, will be to me a tower of strength.

After a delay of a few weeks Parr returned a guilty but final refusal:

> "I had seen only some few of the scattered papers, but of the letter from Queen Elizabeth and the plays I have not seen one syllable.[1] My opinion then was very favourable to the authenticity of what I did see and it was chiefly founded upon internal Evidence. I cannot however conceal from you that some doubts even upon them have been raised in my mind. . . . Of course my judgment is for the present suspended . . . but when I was at Oxford I heard many formidable objections in the conversations of learned men, and upon looking into the Book I met with passages which from the punctuation, orthography, and composition were by no means satisfactory to me. . . . I consider myself as bound by the strictest rules of honour and of morality to weigh all arguments upon all sides, and to yield without reluctance and without dissimulation to their force. I have not read one Controversial Book, and between the contending parties I shall endeavour to preserve the utmost impartiality and candour. I must however confess to you that, as matters stand, I am inclined to suspect the Authenticity of the Plays, and at the same time I am disposed to believe that you have not yourself been deliberately guilty of any imposture. My great object is to discover the truth without any personal predilections or antipathies whatsoever."

This was a serious blow, and it was no consolation for Samuel's friends to assure him that "Dr. Parr always expresses himself strongly, but he sometimes overcharges a picture." But Malone and Steevens still delayed their onslaught, and where Parr had proved traitor others were not so changeable.

[1] Parr had seen the Profession of Faith, the letters to and from Lord Southampton, the letter and verses to Anna, the manuscript of *Lear*, and a number of the smaller papers.

At the beginning of March, Walley Chamberlain Oulton, dramatist and theatrical historian, published *Vortigern under Consideration*, in which he answered Boaden with the spiteful personalities the latter had himself initiated. His own works made Boaden's complaint that the Shakespeare Papers lacked the "glowing diction of poetry" delightfully easy to answer. To quote from one of your rival's plays such a couplet as:

> *"We feel this honour sensibly, my Lord*
> *May we indulge a hope your aunt recovers?"*

And proceed to remark:

> *"From a perusal of the author's works*
> *May we indulge a hope he'll write like Shakespeare?"*

may not be fair argument, but is undeniably effective in controversy, and serves very well to introduce dubious answers to serious criticism. One of Boaden's few effective points had been his claim that the Globe Theatre, at which address Queen Elizabeth had written to Shakespeare, was not then in existence, but was built several years after Leicester's death. Such an allegation had to be answered, and Oulton made up in ingenuity what he lacked in scholarship. "The Theatre in Shoreditch," he argues, "was called the *Curtain*, a name evidently derived from the *stage*, and as the stage is an epitome of the 'Great GLOBE itself'; it is not at all unlikely that Shakespeare should make it the *general* appellation of whatever Theatre he was concerned in—whether on the Bankside or Blackfriars. He himself said: 'all the world's a stage,' and would consequently represent the stage as a *world* in miniature."

About the same time Samuel's friend Wyatt also attacked

James Boaden, and in *A Comparative Review of the Opinions of Mr. James Boaden (editor of the Oracle) in February, March and April, 1795; and of James Boaden, Esq. (author of Fontaineville Forest and of A Letter to George Steevens) . . . relative to the Shakespeare MSS*, overwhelmed the wretched dramatist finally and completely. Boaden's *volte-face* had been whole-hearted and comprehensive. The Papers he now condemned had once filled him with "a tremor of the purest delight" and induced upon his mind a conviction "such as to make all skepticism ridiculous"; while the profession of faith that now had "nothing but the idiomatic poverty and puerile quaintness of a Methodist rhapsody" had once seemed "rationally pious and grandly expressed." Wyatt fails to quote some of the best examples of Boaden's early enthusiasm, such as the paragraph in which he rebuked doubters of the letter to Anna by quoting:

> *"We cannot but remember such things were,*
> *And were most precious to us."*

And declaring that "the man who cannot should never trust himself with the subject of Shakespeare's life; should never by a touch pollute the page of inspiration." But the *Comparative Review* was effective enough to silence its victim for the rest of the controversy.

On the constructive side, Wyatt suffered from the drawback of having a hopeless case, but he possessed sufficient courage frankly to defend the literary merit of the discoveries. The manuscript version of Kent's dying speech "possesses," he says, "sufficient merit to recommend itself to *real* judges of poetry. [The Papers] are not, perhaps, the *most finished* of Shakespeare's production; but they bespeak themselves so truly *his* that (to retort Mr. Boaden's assertion on another occasion), 'he who can believe these lines to be interpolations has neither taste nor sentiment nor discernment in composition.'" His principal argument, like that of Webb, was to claim that the apparent mistakes in the manuscripts must really prove their genuineness. "Would a forger," he asks, "incumber himself with unnecessary letters after the fatal model of Chatterton? Would he not rather have studiously avoided the rock on which that youth split? Would he not follow the *orthography* as carefully as he must have done the *character* of the MSS. of that age?"

But that question has never been satisfactorily answered.

As well as attracting the genuine literary critic, the Papers proved an ideal opening for the hack, the humorist and the would-be author. A pamphlet bearing the most distant reference to the popular topic of the day was sure of a good reception, and new concoctions or old rehashes garnished with a few remarks on the Ireland discoveries were hastily launched on a still unsatisfied market.

By far the best of the parodies was *Precious Relics, or the Tragedy of Vortigern Rehears'd*. The author, who unfortunately still remains anonymous, was clearly well acquainted with Samuel and his supporters, and gives, with a few romantic trimmings, something approaching the true story of the forgeries. Mr. Ireland appears as Dupe, whose son forges the precious relics with the aid of his friend Craft (? Talbot). Sir Isaac Heard and (probably) Francis Webb are at least reflected in Sir Mark Ludicrous and Mr. Wisepate, while Kemble and other actors appear in their own persons. Most of the action takes place at a rehearsal of *Vortigern*:

VORTIMER:

Why this loud clamour? Are the people mad?
That thus, men, women, children, all together
As if ten thousand devils were within them
Make such a hideous cry? Go, stop their voices.

MRS. WISEPATE: Oh do, for heaven's sake.

MR. WISEPATE: Damn it!—Hold your tongue—Must not they make a noise if Shakespeare bid them? Go on Gentlemen.—Don't mind my wife, she is a damned fool.

PROMPTOR: "Stop their voices." That's your cue Mr. Bannister, pray mind your cue.

FOOL: Poo, Mr. Powell, you're mad—fools have no cues, they are all crops!

GENT. IN THE PIT: Very well said Jack—Ha, ha, ha! You're a chip of the old block.

VORTIMER:

Go, stop their voices.

FOOL:

Nay, Prince, though your father's fool I go on no fool's errand.
Stop their voices quoth you; why, there's a better specific at
hand.

VORTIMER:

Out with it then.

FOOL:

Marry, with our hands to stop our ears. Oh, I see the cause of
what we hear—more Saxons are arrived!

VORTIMER:

More Saxons! Has my father then invited
Another and another and another
To make us a new race? Oh shame upon him. . . .

.   .   .   .

VORTIMER:

Out, out vain folly!
Love is an idle fancy, a mere toy
To win·and please an hour before the marriage
And then to charm no more. A theme fit for a novel
Full of darts and cupids, swelling out the volume!

SIR MARK: Egad, that is Shakespeare's style.

DUPE: No one can doubt it. . . .

VORTIGERN:

We give you welcome to our British shore
And would enlarge the gift but have no more
Then, Saxons, take our welcome.

MOB:

We do, we do!

[*Hengist resolves to murder Vortigern.*]

HENGIST:

I'll ask him to a feast, a dinner, at Stonehenge
And he shall dine—but worms shall dine on him;
When at the table he and his are seated,
Then shall the torrent sweep them from their chairs.

DUPE: There, how do you like that, Sir Mark?

SIR MARK: Hem! I don't much approve of the idea of converting a
torrent *into a* sweeping brush.

*DUPE: Oh Sir! It's poetical—consider the inventive genius of our
Bard. But now the murderer enters to receive instructions from Hengist.
I hope Mr. Caulfield is here. Now my dear Mr. C., put on one of your
wicked looks.*

HENGIST:

Here comes my man—he speaks his purpose well
His face is a true index of his mind.
Canst thou cut a throat?

MURDERER:

Aye, windpipe and all.

HENGIST:

Thou hast no scruples?

MURDERER:

Link not fear with murder!

MRS. WISEPATE: Heavens, that fellow makes my blood run cold!

MR. WISEPATE: Poo—in all probability he'll turn king's evidence. . . .

Some of the speeches have the authentic ring of William's more ambitious verse:

> *"Yet there will be a fatal end of all*
> *The roasted oxen, smoking partridges,*
> *The savry venison, the delicious pudding*
> *The luscious fruits, the damask cloth itself,*
> *Yea, all that it contains shall time devour*
> *And, like an alderman for ever greedy,*
> *Leave not a bit behind."*

But, oddly enough, *Precious Relics* attained little popularity.

Typical of the opportunists, who launched their own creative works under cover of the Ireland controversy, is Francis Waldron. A bad actor and a worse writer, Waldron had ambitions that completely outran his abilities. Twenty years before, when he was in his thirties, he had essayed to write a sequel to the *Tempest* that should develop its action and character from where Shakespeare tamely concluded. The attempt had never met any encouragement, but now Waldron seized his opportunity, and under the treacherous title of *Free*

Reflections on Miscellaneous Papers published his long suppressed drama.

He introduces his pamphlet with a few pages of critical jottings against the Papers, observing, for example, that "in the letter to the Earl of Southampton, we read, 'itte is a Budde which Bllossommees Blloomes,' etc. Shakespeare was too good a naturalist not to know that a *Bud* first *Blooms*, then *Blossoms*." But his main concern is not with the Discoveries but with his own work, and, under the borrowed title of *The Virgin Queen*, he devotes the best part of the pamphlet to his Shakespearian imitation.

The verse is very poor stuff, even for the period.

> *"Monster! Stand aloof!"*

cries Miranda to threatening Caliban, who has accompanied Prospero and the others on shipboard:

> *"I feel strange courage and unusual strength*
> *No longer fear thee or thy brutal force*
> *A heavenly inspiration doth assure*
> *No ill shall 'gainst a spotless maid prevail.*
> *The Lybian lion at my feet would crouch*
> *Tho' hunger driven, if what I read be true;*
> *Nor murkiest fiends, nor thou more dreadful yet*
> *Can soil or harm troth-plighted clear virginity."*

This is a fair specimen of the whole wearisome drama.

Although it played but a negligible part in the dispute over the Manuscripts, *Free Reflections* deserves some consideration because its author is so typical of the opposition. Admittedly he used the Ireland controversy solely as the means of his own literary advancement, yet there is no reason to doubt that Waldron sincerely believed the Papers to be forgeries. If this is the case, his attitude must have been based as much upon sentiment or the opinion of his friends as was the vocal belief of the silliest of the supporters. The critical passages in *Free Reflections* display neither scholarship nor historical insight, whilst the *Virgin Queen* proved that its author was wholly lacking in literary taste. Nor was Waldron uniquely deluded about his own talents, for his feeble imitation met sufficient public recognition to be praised in many quarters and republished in the following year. Those who approved and admired such writers as Waldron or Boaden could have no real case against the literary merits of the Shakespeare Papers, and it is significant that none of the opposition condemned the Manuscripts wholly, or even mainly, for their poetic banality.

William was really very unfortunate. Had he possessed greater historical knowledge or enjoyed the help of an antiquarian scholar, he might well have avoided almost all the slips that betrayed him to his contemporaries. A more restrained form of orthography and greater care over dates and modes of address would perhaps have postponed the exposure of the Papers for a good many years; for with nothing to criticise save style, feeling and literary value, most of the opposition would have found little fault with the Manuscripts. But this weakness of taste was not wholly in William's favour. Those who cannot detect the bad will not defend the good with any assurance; the same lack of critical certainty that dare not condemn in face of appearances is equally unwilling to continue to praise in spite of them. The technical errors of the Manuscripts were soon to be exposed so thoroughly that many who still considered them of literary merit dared not defend their convictions against expert hostility. The emotional fervour that originally greeted the Papers was only a froth of sentiment and could not endure in face of serious criticism.

At the beginning of spring, 1796, the controversy was still fairly evenly balanced with, apparently, a slight advantage on the side of the Shakespeare Papers. But whereas Samuel had mustered all his forces, his opponents had yet scarcely come into action, preferring to wait for Malone's long-promised critique and the opening performance of *Vortigern*. "We need not fear," Webb wrote to his friend, "but that we shall ultimately triumph over all opposition. In that thought rest easy, quiet and secure." The advice was easier given than followed; the hour was too late for such facile consolation.

Chapter Eleven

FINAL PREPARATIONS

Having carried his point and obtained the manuscript unconditionally, Sheridan at last began to prepare the production of *Vortigern*, and Samuel looked about him to procure a worthy prologue. At this time the prologue was still an important part of a theatrical presentation. In earlier days the prefatory poem had often been quite unrelated to the play it purported to produce, and might well announce a noble and affecting tragedy with insults, jokes or obscenities. As long as the poem served to arouse the interest or beguile the attention of the audience, its subject was of little moment, and at one time it came to form almost a separate entertainment. By the end of the century the prologue had become a conventional introduction to the play that it preceded, but it still bore considerable weight in determining the mood of the House. The theatres ran very little advance publicity besides posters, playbills and formal announcements in the Press; should a drama be unusual in form or content, its prologue was the easiest means of explaining this fact to the public. *Vortigern* required an introduction that would at once soothe a restive audience, proclaim the play's authenticity, and be worthy of the mighty poet it announced. The obvious man for the job was Henry James Pye, the Poet Laureate.

Pye was perhaps the least suitable of all our unsuitable Laureates. As County Justice, London Police Magistrate, and Member of Parliament for Berkshire he was probably highly efficient, and the verse that he wrote in his leisure hours could not detract from his numerous public services. Unfortunately, these services demanded some recognition, and Pitt must have welcomed the vacant laureateship as the cheapest and most imposing reward for his loyal and poetic supporter. Pye wore his laurels with modesty and determination, and did his poetic duty to the public with the same remorseless competence as he administered justice to criminals. From his appointment in 1790 to his death twenty years later he never ceased to write verse and never began to write poetry.

Pye had long promised to write a prologue for *Vortigern*, and on December 28th he called at Norfolk Street to read the modernised copy of the play. He was much impressed with the drama, and after two hours' study remarked "that he thought it a very excellent play, and wished he could put his name to it as the author." The Laureate agreed with his host that the play must be truly Shakespearian; "there were so many passages in his style and of so much excellence that he could not think it the production of any other person—at the same time he declared that he had shed more tears and had been more affected than at the reading of any play for a long time." Reminded of his undertaking to produce a prologue, Pye replied "with much energy," "that will I do directly, and shall endeavour to produce one that will be worthy of the name of Shakespeare and of the nature of this wonderful discovery."

Ten days passed without word or message, and at last Samuel called at Westminster Police Office to tax Pye with his delay. The poet was a little embarrassed, and after promising to set to work immediately, added with some diffidence: "I have seen Mr. Kemble since I read the Play, and find that in consequence of it I must lower my tone a little with regard to the Prologue, for that opinion strongly differs as to the belief of the Papers being genuine." Mr. Ireland was much put out, and exhorted Pye to remember his position, depend upon his own judgment, and put the presumptuous actor in his place. They parted rather coldly, and it was more than a fortnight later before the Prologue was delivered.

>   *"The cause with learned litigation fraught,"*

sang Pye,

>   *"Behold at length to this tribunal brought*
>   *No fraud your penetrating eye can cheat*
>   *None here can Shakespeare's writing counterfeit.*
>   *As well the tapers base unlustrous ray*
>   *May try to emulate the orb of day,*
>   *As modern Bards whom venal hopes inspire*
>   *Can catch the blaze of his celestial fire.*
>   *If in our scenes your eyes delighted find*
>   *Marks that denote the mighty Master's mind,*
>   *If at his words the tears of pity flow,*
>   *Your breasts with horror fill, with rapture glow,*
>   *Demand no other proof—your souls will feel*
>   *The stamp of Nature's uncontested seal.*
>   *But if these proofs should fail—if in the strain*
>   *You seek the Drama's awful sire in vain,*
>   *Tho' critics, antiquarians, Heralds join*
>   *To give their fiat to each doubtful line,*
>   *Believe them not. Tho' to the nicest eye*
>   *The coiner imitate the Royal dye*
>   *The touchstone soon the error shall unfold,*
>   *Nor let base metal pass for sterling gold.*

This cause then in the last resort you try,
From your tribunal no appeal can lie.
We seek no subtler dye of legal art
Read but the laws of Nature in the heart,
Consult that code from partial favor free
And give, as that decides, your just decree."

This was clearly quite unsuitable. In the first place, the tone was fatally dubious; there were far too many "ifs" and "buts" and "tho's," while such images as that of the coiner were in the worst of bad taste. On the other hand, the approach was not equivocal enough: even to Samuel it seemed highly unwise to let the final verdict on the Manuscripts rest in the hands of a single tumultuous audience.

Samuel sent the Prologue to Francis Webb with a request for his opinion, and was pleased to find his friend in thorough agreement with him:

"I know not Mr. P. but by Character which *in all respects* is in his favour. But as I esteem it a *Duty* to be explicit . . . in all things reflecting this Business, I must freely own, tho' in point of poetic expression I will not venture to criticise, yet in point of *Thought* and *Sentiment* I think it is by no means to be hazarded. I must confess that the general idea is that which would obviously present itself on the first contemplation of the subject. But when we come to consider more minutely the *Whole Business* as it is *peculiarly circumstanced,* and reflect what is hazarded by such an *unreserved Appeal* to this *particular tribunal,* and the *unqualified declaration,* that by the decision on this *one particular, all the rest* must be judged and declared to be *legitimate* or *spurious,* I think with due submission that it is the *last* that should be adopted. 'Tis a nice case and requires more than ordinary skill and delicacy to handle it aright. . . .

If Vortigern were *all*—if this *alone* was in question; if an *unprejudiced* Audience sat in judgment, then the appeal would have been proper and the resolution just. . . .

P.S. I think it right to inform you of a remark made by Miss M. W. with great simplicity, 'one would think,' said she, 'that one of the *other* party had written this Prologue.' "

Strengthened in his disapproval of the poem, Samuel called on Pye and demanded extensive alterations. The Laureate wriggled, apologised, admitted that he had shown the Prologue to Kemble, who had approved it, and finally confessed that "he had a wish to keep on terms with Mr. K., as he had a play then writing on the subject of Henry II which he wished to have brought out at Drury Lane."[1]

In the face of Samuel's justifiable anger at such baseness Pye agreed to alter the offensive passages, and with the other's active co-operation rewrote such objectionable lines as those dismissing the opinions of Herald and Antiquary, and retouched the verse in many small particulars. For the incitement to condemnation that had concluded the original draft Pye substituted:

> *"If on your harrowed soul impressed you feel*
> *The stamp of Nature's uncontested seal*
> *Demand no other proof; nor idly pour*
> *O'er musty manuscripts of ancient lore*
> *To see if every tawny line display*
> *The genuine ink of famed Eliza's day*

[1] The play was finally produced under the title of *Adelaide* in 1800. Kemble played the lead, but even his abilities could not make the piece a success.

Nor strive with curious industry to know
How Poets spelt two centuries ago. . . .

.   .   .   .

But if these proofs should fail; if in the strain
You seek the Drama's awful sire in vain
Condemn not rashly. O'er the forest glade
Tho' the Oak spread no patriarchal shade
Yet may a shrub of no unlovely green
With vivid foliage deck the sylvan scene
Some tuneful notes the vocal woodlands fill
And soothe the air tho' Philomel be still."

And offered to include such a tactful suggestion as:

"If the child's strong and hearty, why engage
With such anxiety about its Sire? . . ."

On the main issue, however, both parties remained un-yielding. Samuel insisted that there should be a direct affirmation of Shakespearian authorship, and on that point alone Pye, with all his anxious readiness to oblige, refused to give way. Finally, faced with the alternative enmities of Samuel or of Kemble, the Laureate chose the safer evil, and, with every expression of regret, resigned to other hands the task of contributing a Prologue.

Samuel was not wholly unprepared for the event. When first Pye began to prove stubborn, he had considered the question of securing another poet, and, as usual, approached Francis Webb with the suggestion that he should take over the honour-able office. Vainly protesting his inexperience, Webb had agreed, and cast his Prologue, as he declared, "rather in a questionable and loose form than in that unequivocal way in which Mr. P. had, in my opinion, inadvisedly done . . . we must give no offence at the threshold."

Webb did the best he could:

> *"How hard the Task on this important Night*
> *With expectation big, to steer aright!*
> *For while we think our polar-star is clear*
> *Some clouds may overcast our Hemisphere! . . .*
> *What counterfeit dare make the rash Essay*
> *To imitate this gem of matchless ray?*
> *Vain were th'attempt to rival Shakespeare's fame,*
> *Impious the fraud to arrogate his name.*
> *On his broad pinions with sun-daring eye*
> *He takes his eagle-flight and mounts the sky,*
> *Exulting leaves all other Bards below*
> *His strength to vindicate, their weakness show. . . ."*

Even Samuel saw the weakness of this brave attempt, and sought the help of Sir James Bland Burges. Sir James was of unimpeachable social standing. His political career, in which he had held the office of Under-Secretary for Foreign Affairs, provided Burke with his memorable dagger, and entertained to dinner the most eminent men of his day, was honourable if not distinguished, and fully deserved the Baronetcy that rewarded and concluded it. Like Pye, his real interests lay outside his profession, and after his retirement in 1795, he was free to devote his leisure to poetry and the drama. A neat Latin rhyme by an anonymous contemporary (perhaps Porson) sums up his poetic talents:

> *"Poetis nos laetamur tribus*
> *Pye, Petro Pindar, parvo Pybus*
> *Si ulterius ire perges*
> *Adde his Sir James Bland Burges."*

which may be translated as:

> "*Three poets praise with plaudits high*
> *Wee Pybus, Peter Pindar, Pye.*
> *If you want weaker lyric urges*
> *Add to the list Sir James Bland Burges.*"

Sir James readily agreed to provide a Prologue for *Vortigern*, and proclaimed himself wholly free from the finnicky objections of the Poet Laureate. "I have no object in view," he wrote to Samuel, "but that of assisting you in the hour of trial; and therefore you may be assured that no fastidious author-like self-love will stand in the way of your criticisms." The poem was promptly delivered and admirably executed, while its author was as good as his word about making alterations. When, on Samuel's recommendation, the lines:

> "*If no effulgent spark of heavenly fire,*
> *No ray divine the languid scene inspire;*
> *If no internal proofs denote its worth*
> *And trace from Avon's banks its happier birth,*
> *With just disdain the dull attempt discard*
> *And vindicate the glory of your Bard.*"

had been deleted, the resulting Prologue seemed in every way satisfactory.

By the middle of March *Vortigern* was in constant rehearsal. Sheridan relented over the scenery, or at least had the vamping done very efficiently, for contemporary reports describe the settings as impressive and even magnificent. But in all other respects the Management behaved as badly as ever, encouraging jeering criticism at the rehearsals, and inciting, or at any rate failing to check, the public hostility of certain members of the cast. Over the advertisements there was open conflict.

Samuel had at first insisted on a direct statement that Shake-speare was the author, but under pressure from his own friends as well as from Sheridan, he agreed to the milder form of "the Play of *Vortigern* discovered among the Shakespearian manu-scripts in the possession of Mr. Ireland." But Sheridan found even this wording too strong, and in spite of his pre-vious agreement advertised simply "a play called *Vortigern*." "The reputation of the Theatre," wrote Samuel angrily, "will not, I presume, be hurt by stating a truth: that the play was written by Shakespeare." But he obtained no redress, and up to the very moment of production had constantly to guard against every sort of treachery. The indisposition that com-pelled Mrs. Siddons to resign her part may have been genuine, but Kemble's proposal to present the play on April 1st was surely dictated by malice. The date of presentation was put forward a day, but the Management still insisted on retaining *My Grandmother* as an inappropriate accompanying farce.[1]

As the opening night approached, Samuel became obsessed with the fear of a pre-arranged plot to damn the piece on its first presentation. Although the idea arose partly from his own imagination, and may have had the unconscious intention of explaining away in advance a hostile reception, yet the increas-ingly clamorous spite of the opposition gave every excuse for the believers to fear the creation of an organised riot. "It has been reported," wrote Wyatt, "that a party is now forming to obstruct the just exercise of public judgment in its decision on the play of King Vortigern (whose merit or demerit it is

---

[1] A musical play by Prince Hoare. It was a peculiarly tactless choice, since the plot was concerned with a foolish art connoisseur who was deceived by the astonishing resemblance between a girl and her dead ancestor.

impossible *that those who have not* seen it can be *acquainted with*) by means of tumult and violence. Should such an attempt so base, so insulting to the understandings of a British audience, be made, it will no doubt be repelled by generous indignation, and will recoil with tenfold shame upon the heads of its conspirators." Samuel was not so sure of a British audience, and sought for means of defence against violent opposition. The best means of checking an uproar was the presence of Royalty in the theatre, and Mr. Ireland wrote to the Prince of Wales requesting his personal attendance in support of the Shakespeare Papers:

"[Mr. Ireland] has reasons to believe a very great Combination is formed with a view to damn the play of Vortigern unheard. Thus injuriously treated, Mr. Ireland feels it a duty he owes to the great literary treasure in his possession, to obtain such a degree of patronage as may counteract the plot of his enemies."

But His Highness regretted that he would probably be away from Town, and hence unable to attend.

Another precaution was to mobilise the Believers, and with that intention Samuel drew up a second and more elaborate Certificate of Belief in the Discoveries:

"We the undersigned having inspected the following deeds in the possession of Mr. Albany Wallis Esq. of Norfolk Street viz.,
A conveyance dated 10 March, 1612, executed to be from Henry Walker to William Shakespeare, William Johnson, John Jackson, and John Heminges of a House in Blackfriars, then or late being in the occupation of one William Ireland; signed William Shakespeare, Jo. Jackson, and Wm. Johnson:

and

A Deed dated 10 February, 1617, being a conveyance signed Jo. Jackson, Wm. Johnson, and John Heming of the same premises:

having also inspected the following papers in the possession of Mr. Samuel Ireland of Norfolk Street, viz:

A MS Play of Lear—a Fragment of Hamlet—a Play of Vortigern—several Deeds witnessed William Shakespeare —several Receipts and Notes of Disbursements of moneys on account of the Globe and Curtain Theatres—familiar letters signed William Shakespeare—and other miscellaneous MSS. And having compared the handwriting of the above Papers in Mr. Ireland's possesions with the signatures of Shakespeare and Hemings to the Deeds in Mr. Wallis's hands— as well as with the published Fac-Similes of the Autograph of Shakespeare to his last will and testament, and to a Deed dated 11 March, 10.JAC.I, which came to the hands of Mr. Wallis about the year 1760 among the Title Deeds of the Rev. Mr. Fetherstonehaugh—and from the character and manner thereof. We declare our firm belief in the Authenticity of the Autograph of Shakespeare and Hemings in the hands of Mr. Ireland.

ISAAC HEARD, GARTER
Having also made a correct copy of the original will of William Shakespeare, and attended to the taking of the Fac-Similes of his signature thereto.
FRANCIS WEBB
ROBERT SHERSON M.D.
HIRAM POWELL
GEORGE FRED. BELT
GILB. FRANKLYN

ALBANY WALLIS
R. TROWARD
JOHN HEWLETT
Translator of Old Latin records, Common Pleas Office.
JOHN BYNG
FRANCIS TOWNSEND
Windsor Herald
MATH. WYATT
JOSEPH SKINNER
R. VALPY."

The signatories to this second Certificate are significantly different from those of the first declaration. Most of those who were of some public repute, whether it was literary, political or merely social, declined to repeat their former open support, and the Scottish peers make a cautious retirement in company with Dr. Parr and James Boswell. There is no reason to suppose that all these supporters had ceased to believe in the Manuscripts; no doubt they sensed the change in popular mood, and realised that what had once promised public esteem now threatened contemptuous notoriety. A curious feature of the affair is the continued belief expressed by the College of Arms. The majority of the Believers can be excused on grounds of technical ignorance, but the Heralds and their clerks, more even than Steevens and Malone, might have been expected to possess a familiar knowledge of ancient writing sufficient wholly to disprove the Shakespeare Papers. In fact, they continued firm in conviction, and this reiteration of their learned support became the strongest argument of Samuel and his adherents.

Actually, the Heralds were not quite as expert as their imposing titles seemed to suggest. The greater part of their work had to do with formal grants and legal documents written in Italian hand; they probably possessed little practical acquaintance with the secretary hand of private correspondence. As legal authorities they were especially impressed by the technical correctness of the Lease and the Deed of Gift; approving their legal phrasing, they forgot to consider the orthography, style or literary value of the Manuscripts. Lastly, there was a purely opportunist motive for acceptance. To express disbelief in documents that Garter King of Arms had publicly acknowledged to be genuine, was both a deliberate affront to a senior officer, and an indiscipline calculated to discredit the College of Heralds itself. As members of a corporate body with a vested interest in ancient manuscripts, the Heralds were bound to maintain complete public accord on matters concerning their office; controversy over the validity of such a discovery would destroy the illusion of unimpeachable certainty that was their principal stock-in-trade. It was better to err as a body than split individually, and when Sir Isaac had taken his stand, his colleagues were compelled to sink their private opinions and follow his example.

The new Certificate did not achieve its purpose, and as April approached the opposition to *Vortigern* became ever louder and more intense. At the last moment even Webb, most faithful of believers, frankly warned his friend of the probable fate of the play, and counselled withdrawal while there was still opportunity:

> "Be not dismayed, Truth must at last prevail. Yield in some sort to the present unpopular scorn or you will be borne down the longer . . . were I in your situation I would at once have an interview with Sheridan, talk freely, and suspend or wholly withdraw the Play. Nor would I have the least objection, in a manly, firm address to the public, to declare the reasons for so doing. . . .
>
> How is your *hidden* friend affected by all this? Will aught prevail on him to come forward in some shape or other to frustrate these bold and infamous Designs? Here's the stop—here we hitch, and here we shall *hang*. Depend upon it, Vort. will not go down. And then where are you?"

But Samuel refused to listen to him.

Four days later, on March 31st, Edmund Malone at last published his attack on the Papers. Now there could be no turning back.

Chapter Twelve

EDMUND MALONE

As soon as Edmund Malone glanced through a copy of *Miscellaneous Papers* he saw with delight that his early hostility was fully justified, and that the manuscripts contained proofs of their own fabrication more plentiful and decisive than his most sanguine hopes could have anticipated. "When I tell your Lordship," he boasted to the Earl of Charlemont, "that in the course of my enquiries I have, with the aid of authentic and indisputable documents, overturned almost every traditional story that has been received concerning Shakespeare for nearly a century past, need I employ many words to shew that I was at least not unconversant with the subject of the late spurious publication? The truth is, that a single perusal of it was sufficient; and in one hour afterwards the entire foundation of the letter I am now writing was laid, and all the principal heads of objection briefly set down." On January 10th he set to work with furious energy to destroy this latest attempt to defame Shakespeare's glory and flout the canonical judgment of his chosen commentator.

Malone had intended to publish his criticism by the middle of February, but as he scrawled sheet after sheet of devastating analysis, enthusiasm took hold of him, and the attack that was originally intended to fill a pamphlet swelled into a lengthy book with an ever receding date of publication. The Believers were jubilant at the delay, taunting their enemy with repentance and incompetence, and even the hostile Press began to remark on his continual postponements. "Mr. Malone," observed the *Morning Herald*, "after having so long threatened to knock the *Shakespearian trunk* to atoms, now says that all his tools are not ready for this curious operation: the *Irelandites*, piquing themselves on this declaration, challenge him to the drawing, and not only deny his power to knock out the *artificial bottom*, but even his ability to discompose a single hair of their favourite *old trunk!*" Malone strongly resented newspaper comment on his affairs, and showed a sufficient dislike of publicity to provoke the sarcasm even of the friendly *Oracle*. "Mr. Malone," remarked Boaden spitefully, "talks rather peevishly of the '*meretricious* and *undesirable* celebrity of a newspaper.' We trust no writer will henceforward offend this fastidious gentleman with anything so irksome to his feeling as *diurnal praise*."

Opposition always incited Malone, and the advance announcement of his forthcoming book was provocative in the extreme:

SPURIOUS SHAKESPEARIAN MANUSCRIPTS

Mr. Malone's detection of this Forgery has been unavoidably delayed by the Engraving having taken more time than was expected, and by some other unforeseen circumstances, but it is hoped it will be ready for publication by the end of this month.

This was much the most downright and unambiguous statement of forgery that had yet been made in the Press, and opened up alarming possibilities of an actual criminal charge. Samuel was seriously disturbed, and eagerly accepted his son's offer to draw up an affidavit exculpating him from complicity in any possible fabrication:

Edmund Malone
From an engraving in the British Museum

AND WHEREAS several disputes have arisen concerning the originality of the Deeds and Manuscript Papers aforesaid. AND WHEREAS EDMUND MALONE of Queen Ann Street East in the Parish of St. Mary le Bone in the said County of Middlesex, has publicly advertised or caused to be advertised an Assertion to the effect that he the said Edmund Malone 'had discovered the above mentioned Deeds and Manuscript Papers to be a forgery,' which assertion may tend in the Event of the said Edmund Malone proving the same, to injure the Reputation of the said deponent's father. Now this Deponent further maketh Oath that he, this Deponent's father, the said Samuel Ireland, hath not nor hath any one of the said Samuel Ireland's family other than, save, and except this Deponent, any knowledge of the manner in which he this Deponent became possessed of the same Deeds or Manscript Papers aforesaid. . . .

William was not formally sworn, as maturer thought suggested that the studied ambiguity of the affidavit might arouse more doubts than its solemn phraseology could dispel. It was decided to publish instead an open letter hinting clearly at the origin of the Papers, and emphasising William's right to have become their possessor. William himself composed the statement:

Mr. Ireland, to satisfy the Public Mind with respect to the Authenticity of these Papers, and at the same time remove every Degree of Suspicion that might attach itself to the Character of the Party who first discovered them, he is authorised to declare that they are by lineal descent the property of a Gentleman whose *Great-Great* Grandfather was a Man of Eminence in the Law into whose possession they fell together with many others relative to Shakespeare, on the Demise of John Heminge's son who died about the year 1650. He is also authorised to state that had it not been for

Mr. S. Ireland Junr. they would have been inevitably lost to the World, the Proprietor himself being totally ignorant of his possessing such a treasure. After this declaration it is supposed that the public are sufficiently gratified and that they are not intitled to any further explanation.

On the following day, March 31st, Malone at last published *An Inquiry into the Authenticity of Certain Miscellaneous Papers and Legal Instruments . . . in a Letter addressed to the Earl of Charlemont.*

Malone had performed his task with the greatest thoroughness, and in four hundred vituperative pages crowded every textual, lexicographic and historical criticism that could be levelled against the Papers. He began by disposing of Mr. H. "The discovery of a title to a considerable estate," he remarks, quoting Samuel's account of the Gentleman's generosity, "must be acknowledged to be so fortunate and beneficial, that one cannot at all wonder at the great liberality of the unknown gentleman on the present occasion, in giving up to the discoverer all his right to these valuable MSS.; but one naturally wishes to know in what county this estate lies, and whether any suit has been instituted within this last year in consequence of this discovery. . . . as the learned Counsel employed by the defendants would, I apprehend, require a more explicit account of the manner and place in which these Deeds were found, than that which has so completely satisfied the profound scholars, antiquaries and Heralds already mentioned." It is typical both of his thoroughness and of his caution that Malone proceeds to quote Gilbert's *Law of Evidence* to show that even if Mr. H. came forward and revealed a convincing pedigree for the Manuscripts it would in no way go to prove their authenticity. Throughout the whole *Inquiry* he strengthens and supports his genuine scholarship with the practised sophistry he had once employed at the Bar.

Samuel, presumably from pleasure at this evidence of Shakespeare's social standing, had given the Letter to Elizabeth pride of place in *Miscellaneous Papers*, and on this letter and its endorsement Malone turned his first and most detailed attack. "It has not been dipped in that stream in which Achilles is said to have been plunged by his mother," he remarks with somewhat self-conscious classicism, "it is, indeed, so far from being vulnerable only in one place, that there is scarcely a single spot in this and all the other papers, in which they are not assailable." In ninety pages of brutal analysis and learned digression he wholly proves his contention.[1]

The orthography was the first and easiest target. Besides denying the existence of such forms as "ande," "forre," and "Londonne," Malone draws up a table comparing four authentic letters of Queen Elizabeth with the one fabricated by William, and shows that no less than twenty-five of William's spellings are contradicated by the genuine examples. Equally fatal to the letter was the would-be archaism of "Hamptowne." "This learned and accomplished Queen," thunders the critic, "who was mistress of eight languages, is here exhibited as such a dolt as not only not to know the true orthography of a word thus familiar to her, but not to be able to distinguish her palace from the neighbouring town; and to

[1] A good many points in Malone's *Inquiry* are inaccurate, as some of his enemies afterwards showed. I shall not indicate them in the present chapter, which is concerned more with the immediate effect of his attack than with its absolute validity.

mend the matter she is made to give to the *town* a termination utterly repugnant to the genus and analogy of the English language. . . ."

So much for the orthography; still more damning was the question of date. The forged letter informed Shakespeare that the Queen was going "toe Hamptowne forre the holy dayes," and commanded him to come "withe thye beste Actorres thatte thou mayste playe before oureselfe toe amuse usse bee notte slowe butte comme toe usse bye Tuesdaye nexte asse the Lorde Leiscesterre wille bee withe usse." Previous critics had remarked the obvious truth that the letter, although undated, must have been written previous to Leicester's death in September 1588. Malone goes on to prove that between December 1585 when Leicester sailed for the Low Countries, and his death three years later, the Queen never spent her holidays at Hampton Court during the months that her favourite was in England. It was impossible to date the invitation previous to 1585, as Shakespeare would scarcely have passed his twenty-first birthday and could not yet have been Manager of a company of Players. And, as Malone points out, Puttenham, writing some years later, does not include him in his list of distinguished poets in spite of such a remarkable instance of the Queen's personal interest.

Against the signatures of Shakespeare, Malone cites the most curious of all his evidences:

"In the year 1766 Mr. Steevens, in my presence, traced with the utmost accuracy the three signatures affixed by the Poet to his Will. While two of these manifestly appeared to us *Shakespere*, we conceived that in the third there was a variation; and that in the second syllable an 'a' was found.

Accordingly we have constantly so exhibited the Poet's name ever since that time. . . . I had no suspicion of our mistake till, about three years ago, I received a very sensible letter from an anonymous correspondent, who showed me very clearly that though there was a superfluous stroke when the Poet came to write the letter 'r' in his last signature, probably from a tremor of the hand, there was no 'a' discernible in that syllable. . . .

"Revolving this letter in my mind, it occurred to me that in the new *fac-simile* of his name which I gave in 1790, my engraver had made a mistake in placing an 'a' over the name, which was there exhibited 'Shakspe^a,' and that what was supposed to be that letter was only a mark of abbreviation, with a turn or curl at the first part of it which gave it the appearance of a letter. I resolved therefore once more to examine the original before I published any future edition of his works; and (it being very material in the present inquiry) to take this opportunity of ascertaining my own error, if any error there was.

"On the 10th March 1612–13, Shakespeare purchased from one Henry Walker a small estate in Blackfriars for one hundred and forty pounds, eighty of which he appears to have paid down; and he mortgaged the premises for the remainder. In the year 1768 the mortgage deed . . . was found by Mr. Albany Wallis among the title deeds of the Rev. Mr. Fetherstonhaugh of Oxted in the County of Surrey, and was presented by him to the late Mr. Garrick. From that deed the *fac-simile* above mentioned was made. As I have not the pleasure of being acquainted with Mrs. Garrick, to whom I was indebted on that occasion, Lord Orford (since I began this Letter), very obligingly requested her to furnish me once more with the deed to which our Poet's autograph is affixed: but that lady, after a very careful search, was not able to find it, it having by some means or other been either mislaid or stolen from her. On the same day on which I received this account I called upon Mr. Wallis, with whom I am acquainted and to whom the deeds of Mr. Fetherstonhaugh, after having been a long time out of his hands, have been lately restored; amongst them he luckily met with the counterpart of the original deed of bargain and sale made on the 10th of March 1612–13, which furnished me with our Poet's name and fully confirmed my conjecture; for there the mark of abbreviation appears at top nearly such as I expected I should find it in Mrs. Garrick's deed, and the Poet having had room to write an 'r,' though on the very edge of the label, his own orthography of his name is ascertained, beyond the possibility of a doubt, to have been SHAKESPERE. . . .

"Notwithstanding this authority, I shall still continue to write our Poet's name SHAKESPEARE, for reasons which I have assigned in his life. But whether in doing so I am right or wrong, it is manifest that he wrote it himself SHAKE-SPERE; and therefore if any original letter or other MS. of his shall ever be discovered, his name will appear in that form. The necessary consequence is that these papers, in which a different orthography is almost uniformly found, cannot be but a forgery."

With a brilliant conjunction of scholarship and spite, Malone ridiculed the rest of the forgeries as thoroughly as he had demolished the Letter from Elizabeth. In a dozen decisive particulars William's meagre learning had failed him. By using Arabic for Roman numerals, by calling Leicester "his Grace," by using a score of anachronistic words, and by giving his heroic ancestor a double Christian name when such a practice was almost unknown, the wretched forger had utterly exposed himself. Concerning the Jacobean Ireland, Malone was especially malicious, and gloatingly informed his readers that the friend whom Shakespeare was said to have loved so dearly, and from whom he had taken the Blackfriars property, was an illiterate haberdasher who could not even sign his own name.

Malone's scholarship was sound, but his opposition to the Papers was based as much upon the nature of their contents as the mode of its expression. A violent anti-Jacobin, he was infuriated by the Republican sentiments attributed to Shakespeare, and saw in William's casual Radicalisms the hidden hand of France; "a country . . . which every friend to the welfare of mankind and peace and the true interest and happiness of England must wish blotted from the map of the world." He especially resented the Poet's slighting reference to "the Gyldedde bawble thatte envyronnes the heade of Majestie," which he denounced as a sentiment whose anachronism was only surpassed by its unworthiness:

"From the present contemptuous mention of KINGS, it is no very wild conjecture to suppose that the unknown writer is not extremely averse to those modern Republican zealots who have for some time past employed their feeble but unwearing endeavours to diminish that love and veneration which every true Briton feels, and I trust will ever feel, for ROYALTY, so happily and beneficially inwoven in our inestimable constitution. . . . The detestable Doctrines of French philosophy and the imaginary Rights of Man had not yet been inculcated; nor had Englishmen been sedulously taught to throw away respect, tradition, form and ceremonious duty, and to accept of *French liberty* and *French equality*, instead of that beautiful and salutory gradation of ranks which forms an essential part of our admirable constitution; where the distinction of conditions is so easy and imperceptible, that almost every man under the first personages of the land classes himself, in his own estimation, without offence, in a somewhat higher order than that to which he is strictly entitled."

Some of the reviews jeered at Malone's constitutional fervour. "Mr. Malone's attack on the French Revolution," commented one of the journalists, "may be accounted for on the philosophical principle of *the association of ideas,* as laid down by Hartley. He was employing his mind on *antiquated* and *musty* manuscripts; this recalled to his recollection, by the law of resemblance, his own *antiquated* and *musty* prejudices." But for all the critic's exaggerations he had made a very important point, and in showing that Shakespearian England was not democratic, not shocked by war, and not much troubled about the personal liberty of the lower orders, he exposed one of the many emotional anachronisms of the Forgeries.

"I have now done," concluded Malone, summing up his *Inquiry*, "and I trust I have vindicated Shakespeare from all this 'imputed trash,' and rescued him from the hands of a bungling imposter, by proving all his manuscripts to be the true and genuine offspring of consummate ignorance and unparalleled audacity." The *Inquiry* was patently prejudiced and vindictive; it was verbose and not entirely free from factual errors. But the culminative effect was overwhelming, and the five hundred copies sold in the two days before the production of *Vortigern* must have carried more weight than the sum of all the preceding pamphlets. Samuel's wild allegations that Malone was personally organising a riot were quite untrue; his book had made a more active intervention totally unnecessary.

Chapter Thirteen

THE FIRST NIGHT OF "VORTIGERN"

Samuel looked forward to the opening night of *Vortigern* with the greatest apprehension. At any performance, an eighteenth-century audience could be rowdy and riotous enough; on special occasions when excitement was running high it required but the slightest stimulus to provoke pandemonium or pitched battle. Should the House dislike a play or a performer, they interrupted mercilessly with voice or even missile, and the same enthusiasm that had been known to reduce the pit to fits of genuine hysterics could, on other occasions, incite heartless mockery of the most moving tragedy. Sometimes excitement became panic, and panic, disaster. Two years before, at a royal command performance, the crowd's rush down the narrow stairs of the pit became a wild stampede in which fifteen people, including the King's two Heralds, were knocked down and trampled to death. It may have disturbed the more superstitious of the Believers to remember that on that occasion, too, *My Grandmother* had been part of the programme.

Samuel's fear of organised opposition was not unreasonable, for planned interruption of unpopular plays was by no means an uncommon practice. Tailors, fancying an insult to their trade, had broke up a Benefit performance of *The Tailors, A Tragedy for Warm Weather*; patriotic mobs had howled down Garrick for appearing with Swiss actors during a war with France; and, in 1809, when Covent Garden raised its pit charges from three and six pence to four shillings, the performances were systematically howled down for sixty-seven nights until the old prices were restored. The public's excitement was often the producer's disaster.

The opening night of *Vortigern* promised a record house. Doors were opened at five-thirty for a performance an hour later, but at three o'clock there was already a queue, and by half past four the streets around the theatre were packed by the waiting crowd. As the people thronged to the entrances, they were met by dozens of shouting boys who thrust into their hands *Vortigern's* last defence:

VORTIGERN

A *malevolent* and *impotent* attack on the Shakespeare MSS having appeared, on the *eve* of representation of the play of *Vortigern*, evidently intended to injure the interest of the proprietor of the MSS, Mr. Ireland feels it impossible, within the short space of time that intervenes between the publishing and the representation, to produce an answer to the most illiberal and unfounded assertions in Mr. Malone's *'Inquiry'*; he is, therefore, induced to request that the play of *Vortigern* may be heard with that *candour* that has ever distinguished a *British Audience*.

But the audience had come to enjoy itself.

The signal for admission started a stampede. Both the pit and the boxes had been sold out in advance, but the crush round the pit entrance was so savage that many ticket holders paid the box price for the privilege of dropping down to their seats from inside the theatre. The two-shilling gallery was stormed and the doorkeepers thrown aside—very few of the entrants can have paid for their seats. A member of the audience remarked that there were fewer than twenty women in the pit, a striking evidence of the savagery of the rush. The House must have been almost a record one, for more than two thousand five hundred people paid for admission.

The feeling of the audience seemed to be divided. When Samuel took his seat in a centre box he was applauded from the gallery (where he had been allotted forty complimentary tickets), and jeered only from a small section of the pit. But the atmosphere was dangerously tense, and William, who had the strongest forebodings of failure, declined to sit with his father in the seats of honour, and spent the performance behind the scenes in the Green Room. The Prologue was spoken by Mr. Whitfield:

> *"No common cause your verdict now demands*
> *Before the Court immortal Shakespeare stands . . ."*

he began, and was greeted with catcalls and shouts of disapproval that continued for some minutes before he could again make himself heard:

> *"That mighty Master of the human soul*
> *Who rules the passions, and with strong control*
> *Through every turning . . . through every . . ."*

Poor Whitfield, unnerved by his reception, broke down, and in spite of the prompter's urgent whispers could not go on. Voices in the audience shouted encouragement, and after assuring his hearers that nervousness and not forgetfulness had made him falter his lines,[1] he was able to continue without further mistakes:

---

[1] Every eighteenth-century actor was anxious to avoid the charge of not knowing his part, for although performers were occasionally allowed astonishing licence, a bad memory might incite playgoers to a permanent hostility.

" . . . *From deep oblivion snatch'd, this play appears:*
It claims respect, since Shakspeare's name it bears;
That name, the source of wonder and delight,
To a fair hearing has at least a right.
We ask no more—with you the judgment lies;
No forgeries escape your piercing eyes!
Unbiass'd, then, pronounce your dread decree,
Alike from prejudice and favour free.
If, the fierce ordeal pass'd, you chance to find
Rich sterling ore, tho' rude and unrefin'd,
Stamp it your own; assert your poet's fame,
And add fresh wreaths to Shakspeare's honour'd name."

The conclusion of the Prologue was received with prolonged
applause, intended, no doubt, as much for the speaker as for its
sentiments, and the audience settled back to give *Vortigern* its
fair hearing.

The plot of *Vortigern* was derived from Holinshed, but
William had taken a good many liberties with the story. Old
Constantius, King of Romanised Britain, much troubled by
the invasions of the Picts and Scots, seeks the help of his
ambitious general, Vortigern, "in all respects a most vicious
character," as the *True Briton* justly observed, and takes him
into Royal partnership. Vortigern's furious ambitions are not
content with the mere exercise of power, and, after a very brief
struggle with his conscience, he has the old King murdered,
blames the deed on Scottish emissaries, and assumes the crown
himself. Aurelius and Uter, Constantius' two sons, are at
Rome when the murder takes place, and hearing that Vortigern
seeks their lives also, flee to Scotland to seek protection and
raise an army against the usurper. Meanwhile, Vortigern has
sought the help of Hengist and Horsus, the Saxon princes.

With Hengist is his daughter Rowena, who so captivates Vortigern, that for her sake he insults and divorces his wife Edmunda and disowns his children. The Britons rebel, the Saxons are defeated, Hengist and Horsus are slain, and Aurelius, after sparing Vortigern's life, becomes King of England. Interwoven with the main story are a number of sub-plots, including the love of Flavia, Vortigern's daughter, for Aurelius, and her wanderings in the forest dressed as a man. William claimed that he wrote the part especially for Mrs. Jordan in the same way that he intended Vortigern for Kemble, and, perhaps because the part was so perfectly suited to the actress, these pastoral scenes were much the most popular feature of the play. In the original story, and in William's first draft, there was reference to Vortigern's incestuous love for his daughter. But the Lord Chamberlain allowed no licence even to Shakespeare, and removed the offending passages.

The audience probably knew the outline of the plot, but no one save Samuel and a few of his friends had read the play itself. The curtain rose to considerable applause, and revealed Constantius enthroned in state, surrounded by his barons:

CONSTANTIUS: *Good Vortigern! as peace doth bless our isle,*
And the loud din of war no more affrights us,
And as my soul hath plac'd thee next herself,
'Tis our desire that thou deny'st us not
That, which anon we crave thee to accept;
For though most weighty be the proffer'd task,
We trust thy goodness will the toil accept,
Since we have always found thee kind by nature;
And, as the pelican, e'en with thy blood,
Ready to succour and relieve.

VORTIGERN: *Most gracious sov'reign! to command is thine;*
And, as a subject, mine is to obey.

CONSTANTIUS: *Such was the answer we did here expect,*
And farther now we shall explain our meaning:—
As frozen age we find doth fast approach,
And state affairs lie heavy with ourself,
To thee one half our pow'r we here resign,
That due reward may pace with thy great labour.
To this our proposition what reply? . . .

William had no patience with slowness of action or development, and it required but a very few lines for Vortigern to have planned and arranged his master's murder:

VORTIGERN: *Now then good King prepare thee for the worst.*
For ere the thick and noisome air of night
Shall with damn'd Hecate's baneful spells be fill'd,
Thou must from hence to the cold bed of death,
To whom alike peasant and king are slaves,
Come then black night, and hood the world in darkness,
Seal close the hearts of those I have suborn'd,
That pity may not turn them from their purpose.   [Exit.]

CONSTANTIUS: *O sleep, thou nourisher of man and babe,*
Soother of every sorrow, thou can'st bury
The care-distracted mind in sweet oblivion,
To thee, O gentle pow'r I pawn my soul!
Here then, on my bended knee, great God,
Let me implore thy grace, and look for mercy;
[Though thou hast plac'd me sovereign over men,
And on my brow hath fix'd a diadem;
Yet am I subject still to human frailty,
And naught can boast more than thy meanest vassal.][1]
How wisely hast thou fram'd thy work of nature,

---

[1] These four lines were omitted at the performance, presumably for their apt reference to another monarch.

Even the smallest reptile hath its instinct
Aye, is as nicely form'd as man himself.
Both too must die, both rot and come to dust.
Yet man hath one great property besides,
A never fading, an immortal soul!
Upon that thought I rest my happiness.

As he wrote the play William had apparently become increasingly confident of his own powers, and from scene to scene he gradually progresses from the pedestrian to the pretentious, and from the pretentious to the almost absurd. In the latter scenes of the first Act he is still careful, but clearly beginning to get into his stride:

VORTIGERN: *Oh! my thrice noble and right worthy Peers,*
We are now met upon the heaviest summons
That ever yet did occupy our thoughts;
The sparkling drop which graces every eye,
And fain would deluge every manly cheek,
Denotes the brimful sorrow of each heart;
Pity disgraces not the manly brow,
And yet it suits but ill the present crisis,
When our best strength and wisdom both are needful,
To stem this black, this damn'd conspiracy;
For bloody war and foul rebellion lurk
Beneath the mask of cruel treachery,
Which i' the present is so plainly shewn,
By the brutal deed of these vile Scotsmen!
Then let not drowsy thought deter our purpose,
Nor basely rot in us the plant of justice,
The clamorous people call aloud for sentence,
Should we delay, it will go hard with us.

FIRST BARON: *Trusting to thee, our noble good Protector,*
We do, without delay, pronounce as guilty,
The perpetrators of this crying deed.

We also do, with general accord,
Beseech you bear the office of a King,
Until the Princes do return from Rome;
For on Aurelius, now the elder son
Of our deceased King the election lights;
Well do we know how tedious is this task,
How full of trouble and perplexity!
But we do also know thee for a man,
Most good, most perfect, and most merciful!

VORTIGERN: *I fear good Barons you do flatter me!*
I thought ere this, to have resigned the weight,
Which the late King had heap'd upon my shoulders;
But mark the sad reverse, for even now,
You double this my load, and bear me down;
Oh! you ha' struck me where I am indeed
Most vulnerable—The voice o' th' people!
For them I will surrender liberty. . . .

William's poetic gifts, such as they were, found their best
expression in tragic thunder and the clamorous periods of high
melodrama. In lighter modes his invention failed him, and in
the pastoral of Act II, "murder most foul," "aching heart,"
"minister of mercy," "balm of comfort," "smiling joy," the
"sooty mantle" of night, and the "eternal sleep of death"
crowd together in platitudinous procession. Perhaps the very
platitude of the verse appealed to the audience, for the
curtain fell on the second Act to considerable applause, and
for a moment William imagined that the play might be a
success.

Trouble began in the third Act when the players,
intentionally or by accident, began to incite the noisy
humour of the audience. The Act opened with an assembly

of Barons, and the verse resounded with the clamour of the trumpet:

FIRST BARON: *Girt tight the drums, and sound yon brazen trumpet,*
Let it proclaim aloud our firm decree:
Aurelius and his brother both are traitors,
And 'gainst their mother country do rebel.

[Trumpet sounds]

SECOND BARON: *Nay, stop not there; but let them bellow on*
Till with their clamorous noise they shame the thunder.

The part of the Second Baron had been given to Charles Dignum, a very clumsy actor possessed of a fine tenor voice. His cry, "let them bellow on," was delivered in a high-pitched musical tone, and brought such a roar of laughter and applause that the play was held up several minutes until Kemble came forward to ask for silence. The rest of the Act, helped out by songs, went off without further disturbance, but the audience's appetite for amusement was aroused, and it was not long before others of the cast began to behave in the manner their patrons evidently expected.

In the fourth Act there was battle between Scots and Saxons, and Horsus was killed in single combat. The part of the Saxon general had been unsuitably allotted to "the late facetious Mr. Phillimore, of *large-nosed* memory," and he took the occasion of his death-scene to play up to his reputation. "That gentleman," writes William in his *Confessions*, "on receiving the deadly wound (which proved, indeed a deadly blow to my play), either from prior tuition or chance (I will not pretend to decide which) so placed his unfortunate carcass that on the falling of the drop-curtain he was literally divided between the audience and his brethren of the sock and buskin; his legs etc. being towards the spectators, and his head etc. inside the curtain, which concealed them from observation. This, however, was not the only calamity: for as the wooden roller at the bottom of the curtain was rather ponderous, Mr. Phillimore groaned beneath the unwelcomed burden; and finding his brethren somewhat dilatory in extricating him, he adopted the natural expedient of extricating himself. . . ." The applause and laughter that had greeted Phillimore's writhings became complete pandemonium when it was seen that Charles Sturt, M.P., an ardent believer, was drunkenly trying to drag the actor into his stage box.

Excited by the death of Horsus the audience became increasingly restive, interrupting the florid speeches and commenting noisily on the more obvious borrowings from other plays. Disturbance came to a head in the fifth Act, when Vortigern, surrounded by his enemies, harangues Death and Conscience in William's most lurid style. This was the big scene of the play, and Kemble ranted furiously about the stage:

> "*Time was, alas! I needed not this spur.*
> *But here's a secret, and a stinging thorn,*
> *That wounds my troubled nerves, O! conscience! conscience!*
> *When thou didst cry, I strove to stop thy mouth,*
> *By boldly thrusting on thee dire ambition.*
> *Then I did think myself indeed a god!*
> *But I was sore deceiv'd, for as I pass'd,*
> *And travers'd in proud triumph the Basse-court,*
> *There I saw death clad in most hideous colours,*
> *A sight it was that did appal my soul.*
> *Yea, curdled thick this mass of blood within me.*

Full fifty breathless bodies struck my sight,
And some with gaping mouths did seem to mock me,
Whilst others smiling in cold death itself,
Scoffingly bad me look on that, which soon
Wou'd wrench from off my brow this sacred crown,
And make me too a subject like themselves;
Subject! to whom? To thee, O sovereign death!
Who hast for thy domain this world immense;
Church-yards and charnel-houses are thy haunts,
And hospitals thy sumptuous palaces,
And when thou would'st be merry, thou dost chuse
The gaudy chamber of a dying King.
O! then thou dost ope wide thy hideous jaws,
And with rude laughter, and fantastic tricks,
Thou clap'st thy rattling fingers to thy sides;
And when this solemn mockery is ended,
With icy hand thou tak'st him by the feet,
And upward so, till thou dost reach the heart,
And wrap him in the cloak of lasting night."

What actually happened is obscure. According to William the House seized on the unfortunate line "and when this solemn mockery is ended" to break into irrepressible tumult. "No sooner was the above line uttered in the most sepulchral tone of voice imaginable, and accompanied with that peculiar emphasis which on a subsequent occasion so justly rendered Mr. Kemble the object of criticism (viz. on the first representation of Mr. Coleman's Iron Chest)," he writes in his *Confessions*, "than the most discordant howl echoed from the pit that ever assailed the organs of hearing. After the lapse of ten minutes the clamour subsided; when Mr. Kemble, having again obtained a hearing, instead of proceeding with the speech at the ensuing line, very politely, and in order to amuse the audience still more, re-delivered the very line above quoted with even more solemn grimace than he had in the first instance displayed."

This is the popular story, but like so much contained in the *Confessions*, it appears to have little foundation in fact. In spite of William's claim that the incident was obvious to the whole audience and was probably "the *watchword* agreed upon by the Malone faction for the general howl," none of the reviews, save only that in *The Times*, makes any comment on the line in question. The Press generally agree that uproar finally supervened during or soon after this speech, but it seems very improbable that Kemble could have behaved in so blatant a fashion without exciting any unfavourable comment. No doubt Kemble, perceiving the growing disorderliness of the audience, and unwilling to be the target of their active antagonism, decided to show his real sympathies by deliberately guying the whole speech. Fancying himself as a comedian, it is more than probable that he made a few solemn grimaces and over-acted just sufficiently to incite the rowdier elements of the House; the studied repetition that William describes would have been quite unnecessary. But whatever his private convictions Kemble was merely an employee, and when the shouting threatened to drown the rest of the performance he came forward and appealed for silence: "Ladies and Gentlemen, allow me to remind you that the title to authenticity which this play lays claim to depends on your giving it a fair and full hearing." Coming from Kemble the request was fairly effective, and the rest of the play was heard in comparative order. When the curtain fell the booing was mixed with applause that cannot have been wholly ironical.

The Epilogue was spoken by Mrs. Jordan. Samuel had

wisely rejected the partisan verses of the original draft[1] in
favour of something a little less provocative; and when their
favourite, still wearing her boy's habit, winsomely recited:

> *"You're all, whate'er you think, his characters.*
> *How!—do you doubt it?—cast your eyes around,*
> *In ev'ry corner of this house they're found.*
> *Observe the jolly grazier in the pit,*
> *Why, he is Falstaff, fat, and full of wit;—*
> *In fun and feasting places his delight,*
> *And with his Dolly emulates the Knight.*
> *Look at that youth, whose countenance of woe*
> *Denotes a tender-hearted Romeo;*
> *He only wishes, tho' he dare not speak,*
> *To be a glove to touch his Juliet's cheek;*
> *While she, from yonder terrace, smiles serene,*
> *And longs with him to play the garden scene.*
> *But O! I tremble now,—there sits a man,*
> *Rugged and rough, a very Caliban!*
> *He growls out his displeasure—'tis a shame!*
> *Do, dear Miranda, make the monster tame.*
>
> . . . .
>
> *'Tis true, there is some change, I must confess,*
> *Since Shakespeare's time, at least in point of dress.*
> *The ruffs are gone, and the long female waist*
> *Yields to the Grecian more voluptuous taste;*
> *While circling braids the copious tresses bind,*
> *And the bare neck spreads beautiful behind.*
> *But, for the cloak and pointed beard we note*

[1] *Shall then at length irreverent Doubt prevail,*
And dare your favourite Shakespeare to assail,
Reject each proof that candour can supply
And what it cannot controvert, deny:
While none from censure's blast his flower shall save
Posthumous flowers, the Garland of the Grave?"
etc., etc.

The close-cropt head, and little short great-coat.
Yet is the modern Briton still the same,
Eager to cherish, and averse to blame;
Foe to deception, ready to defend,
A kind protector and a gen'rous friend."

the pit rewarded her with prolonged applause.

But appreciation of the Epilogue was not approval of the play, and an attempt to announce *Vortigern* for the following night was received with a storm of catcalls and scuffling that continued unabated for a quarter of an hour, until Kemble came forward and promised instead the ever popular *School for Scandal*. Many of the believers expressed their disapproval at this decision, and the invincible Sturt pelted the actor with apple parings. But the noisier parts of the audience were well satisfied, and when the curtain fell Samuel saw clearly that he could never produce the play again. "How many persons," asked Pye, "were there in the theatre that night who, without being led, could distinguish between the merits of King Lear and Tom Thumb? Not twenty," and in some quarters it was claimed that supporters of the Manuscripts had actually been in the majority at the fatal performance. But the opposition, more assured, vocal and determined, shouted *Vortigern* into oblivion.

Samuel and his son went home together immediately after the Epilogue. Samuel sat up most of the night with his friends, discussing what best to do to preserve his own credit and that of the Papers. But William slept early and well, feeling, as he afterwards said, "more easy in my mind than I had been for a great length of time, as the load was removed which had oppressed me."

Chapter Fourteen

WILLIAM LOSES HIS HEAD

If William was easy in his mind, his father was exceedingly unhappy. On April 3rd Samuel called at Drury Lane to collect his share of the takings, and received £102 13s. 3d., £30 of which he gave to his son.[1] But a hundred pounds odd was poor compensation for universal obloquy; for the collapse of *Vortigern* had encouraged rather than satisfied the enemies of the Manuscripts, and on all sides Mr. Ireland was openly accused of their fabrication. It was clear to his friends that unless Samuel could reveal the source of the Discoveries, and by so doing either prove their authenticity or shift the odium of forgery on to other shoulders, he would probably be hounded to ruin by that ruthless vindictiveness that was so marked a characteristic of the age of reason. "It was what I expected and what I indicated," wrote Francis Webb of the performance of *Vortigern*, "though I have no doubt of much *foul play* in every sense of the word. I will give you my opinion freely, which is: that only if your concealed friend will come forward, assure the whole, or afford other matter (which perhaps will be difficult) that will put suspicion itself to silence; it would be vain to attempt to prove credit with the public by any other means than those already us'd. And I must honestly declare, as I have to Sir Isaac *in confidence*, that unless this be done I shall not [understake], in any respect whatever, to engage further than I have already done. You repeatedly said your hidden friend would in due time come forward. What has kept him

[1] He had already given William £60 of the advance payment.

back? If he is not in some shape or other forthcoming, I must confess I shall entertain suspicions which I once thought it impossible would ever have entered my mind. . . ."

In vain did Mr. Ireland bully and beseech his son to bring forward the mysterious Gentleman; William remained ";rude and silent," and would answer nothing. On April 9th, Samuel wrote an imploring letter to Montague Talbot:

"I now take up the Pen on a subject, my good Sir, the most painful and oppressive that I have ever been engaged in in the Course of my Life, a matter of no less consequence than that of the happiness of myself and family, and perhaps may terminate in my ruin. I need not say that this subject is the Shakespeare MSS. which thro' your original Discovery came to my son, and from him into my possession. The originality of them has been doubted by some and totally disbelieved by many. The source of these doubts has been from the mysterious way in which they were first discovered, and from my total inability to give the Public any satisfaction on that head. When I received them, I applied to various persons whom I had reason to believe were skilled in the various branches of knowledge necessary to give a sanction to the belief or disbelief of their originality. These opinions being favourable to the latter, together with the full conviction on my own part both from their appearance and the manner in which they came to my hands, as being from my son who I cannot imagine would be so base as to involve me and his family in infamy and ruin by becoming an accesory with any person or persons in putting forth an imposition.

"Thus situated I have laid some of them before the Public, which have been but ill received and on which I have sustained a pecuniary loss. The play of *Vortigern* has likewise been presented and has met with a fate that has involved me still further in inconvenience. I have been abused publicly and privately for such an attempt to impose on the Town, and I hear the public determination is to pursue me even to ruin. This I cannot but feel most acutely, as being totally ignorant of having done anything injurious. I feel it therefore incumbent on you, and indeed a duty that you owe to my injured family, to give some relief on this occasion, and to stand forward in some way or other to exculpate me from the Infamy that at present I inadvertently lay under. . . . I beg to inform you that I do not at all consider you as accessory to my publishing these Papers, but as they came through you I hope and trust you will in some way render me the justice to exculpate me from any intention of doing ill, or should it be a forgery, which I think impossible, exonerate me from being at all an accomplice in the business. . . ."

Talbot was placed in a difficult position. He had no wish to betray his friend (doubtless he realised, too, that the truth might not be credited), but he had not the least intention of entering on further deception that might end in a criminal charge. In this emergency, however, his subtlety did not desert him, and, as on a previous occasion, he showed his mastery of an awkward situation. He could never, replied Talbot, break his solemn vow to respect the Gent's anonymity; that was a secret he would preserve in face of death itself. But he sympathised with Mr. Ireland in his miserable predicament, and suggested a course that would at least clear him from suspicion of forging the Manuscripts. He proposed that William and himself should make a solemn affidavit that no one save themselves and Mr. H. knew the secret of the Papers, and that Samuel was totally ignorant of their history and origin. Talbot's only condition was that William should join him in swearing such a declaration. This was a highly ingenious move. The affidavit would satisfy Samuel by clearing him of responsibility, but at the same time was impossible for William to swear since it amounted to an oath that Mr. H. really existed. William was bold enough in the ordinary way, but in face of the dreadful penalties for detected perjury he dared not agree to swear. Talbot, naturally, refused to act alone, and William was left to bear the full brunt of his father's rage and reproaches.

Meanwhile Samuel's friends had pursued another mode of enquiry, and set up a Committee of Investigation into the source of the Papers and the identity of their donor. The first meeting of the Committee was on April 14th, and William drew up a statement for his father to read to the company:[1]

"The Gentlemen are to be informed where the Papers came from, the Gentleman's name, to whom they belong, and who discovered by, and in what place and manner. The schedule of those which remain behind is in my father's possession, which he may show, and will likewise be accounted for by me.

S. W. H. IRELAND."

The schedule (which William had written in light-headed triumph after the incident of the Heming autograph) was a truly remarkable document. Besides the treasures already shown to the world the Gentleman possessed the complete manuscripts of *Richard II, Henry II* and *Henry V*; and incomplete manuscripts of *Othello, King John, Richard III, Timon of Athens, Julius Cæsar* and *Henry IV*. In addition to the plays, Mr. H.

---

[1] The list of members at this meeting is given as: Bacon, Bland Burges, Gilbert Franklyn, Hewlett, Newton, Townsend, Byng, Parnell, Wallis, Wyatt, Hastings and the Rev. Warburton, Chaplain to the Archbishop of Canterbury.

had Shakespeare's own catalogue of his library, his Deed of
Partnership in the Curtain Theatre, original verses to Francis
Drake, Sir Walter Raleigh, Lord Howard and Queen Elizabeth; as well as the whole-length portrait and the miniature set
in silver that had already been described. Most of these wonders
William had actually seen, but the Gentleman had also
described to him hundreds of priceless books containing Shakespeare's signature, and a brief account of his life written in the
Poet's own hand. Much impressed by the remarkable revelations, the Committee drew up a joint letter to be delivered to
Mr. H.:

> "A meeting of gentlemen for the purpose of taking into
> consideration the obloquy under which Mr. Ireland labors in
> consequence of his presentation of the Shakespeare MSS,
> are desirous of knowing whether the gentleman from whom
> Mr. Samuel Ireland received the said MSS be disposed to
> lend his assistance towards rescuing them from the state of
> doubt in which they now stand with the Public."

The Gentleman expressed his willingness to be of assistance,
and with William's assent it was decided to make a list of
twelve distinguished men, two of whom Mr. H. should select
to be the repositories of his invaluable secret.

The Committee had splendid ideas, and at their second
meeting in the following week they drew up a panel of the
most dazzling celebrities. Mr. H. was offered his pick of two
dukes, four earls, two bishops, the Speaker and a sparkling
array of politicians from which he might choose his confidants;
and although none of these notables had yet been informed of
the duty for which he was destined, their acquaintances on the
Committee assured each other that no one would refuse the

honour of so important a commission. Almost alone of these inflated investigators Byng kept his sense of proportion, and from his country retreat at Biggleswade wrote Samuel a sensible and appealing letter:

> When I parted from you yesterday I felt a very different opinion from the majority of the meeting. For altho' it may be wished that two Persons of high Rank, men of Literature, should visit the Gentleman (and vouch accordingly); yet I must think that to all such applications you will either receive no answer, or else a decided negative. Most of these *high* gentlemen have either been indifferent, or professed Scoffers of the MSS.
>
> Whatever, then, more is done to the advantage of the MSS, can only be done by your old Friends; and by two of them, at last, will this *Gentleman* be seen.
>
> The Repetition of your Meetings will draw together Spies, Enemies and others from curiosity. It certainly might do good if two Dukes or Statesmen would take the matter in hand. But they will not. . . .
>
> You know and believe my constancy. But listen not at all to the new Comets. Were I thought worthy of being one of the Embassy (when the Nobility and Literati shall have declined) I would return to Town upon the Spot.
>
> Your son, when I dined with him yesterday, again told me that I should recognise *the Gentleman* at the first sight!!
>
> Wishing you success, I am,
Yrs
J. B.

Byng's forecast proved entirely correct; the "new Comets," on every ground and none, refused to tarnish their glory with the mud of a literary controversy, and the investigation was left to Samuel's old acquaintances. At the beginning of May "Mr.

George Chalmers . . . with some reluctance accepted the charge of receiving the secret conjointly with Mr. Byng . . . but in a few days, understanding that Mr. Byng was objected to by the Gent., as my son said, because he was on the Committee and, besides, a sworn friend to myself and to the Papers—it was determined to apply to Mr. Wallis. He said he would as a professional man take the secret to himself, but would not jointly with any further person have anything to do with it, not being able to answer for the secrets of any other person."

William eagerly accepted the proposal, and Whit-Sunday, May 17th, was appointed as the day for revealing the secret. At last Samuel had a chance of seeing Mr. H., and he determined not to miss his opportunity. "I, not being desirous of having it known that I was present," he afterwards noted, "I went to Mr. Francillon's opposite to Mr. Wallis'—when Mr. F. and I waited at the first floor window to see him come, but principally to see if there was any Gentleman that I might recognise his person. Sam [William] came at the appointed time, but no appearance of any Gent. and only one person that I could suspect, and him I begged Mr. Francillon's servant might, after he came out, follow; which he did, and he was found to be an indifferent person. After waiting at the window about an hour after he went out, Sam came from Mr. Wallis', and a short time after, I went over and questioned Mr. Wallis as to what had passed, to which he would make no satisfactory answer. For several days after this I called on Mr. Wallis, but not getting anything from him I was led to suspect that my son had been prevailing on Mr. W. to believe that he was Author of the Papers (a circumstance that he had several times had the arrogance and vanity to declare to all the family, but never was bold enough to say so much to me)." While his father peered hopefully from the opposite window, William had frankly and fully confessed the whole secret of the Shakespeare Papers.

The behaviour of Albany Wallis is exceedingly curious. William confessed under pledge of secrecy, and it was no doubt proper that the lawyer should respect even such a confidence as this. But Wallis did more than suppress the truth, for before very long he hinted at further imaginary secrets and actually encouraged Samuel to believe in the existence of a mysterious donor from whom the Manuscripts had been obtained. When William himself made public admission of the forgeries and begged his confidant to substantiate the confession, Wallis still refused to make a definite statement, and even concealed the fabrications that William had specially produced as specimens of his capabilities as a forger. "Mr. Wallis' conduct in this respect," wrote William some time afterwards, "seems to me very extraordinary, as I several times begged that he would tell my father that all the *secret* he heard from me was an avowal of my being the author of all the Papers. By not doing this he has enabled my father to throw a doubt on the affair by giving the world to understand he suspects some other *secret* being divulged to Mr. Wallis." Albany Wallis was less of a legal adviser than an unwanted accomplice.

There are several possible explanations of the lawyer's curious conduct. His most obvious motive would seem to be simple vanity. As long as he held the secret he was a person of great importance, enjoying the flattering attention of Samuel and the Believers; and he may well have been tempted to exaggerate the strangeness of his knowledge in order to make a more profound impression. When William publicly confessed to forging the Papers, Wallis may have found himself committed to a story much more exciting than the real truth, and dared not confess to Samuel that it was merely the product of his own self-conceit.

Another possibility is that Wallis was somehow concerned in the forgeries and had prior knowledge of the whole affair. He certainly took no part in the actual fabrication; William, as many witnesses testified, was skilled in the technical production of the Papers, while their literary and historical content is clearly too crude and inaccurate to have been the work of an accomplished antiquary. In any event, the Manuscripts are so wholly in tune with William's mind and imagination that it is impossible to believe them the work of any other person. Nevertheless, Wallis may have known William's secret a good while before the beginning of the investigation. Personally, I am almost convinced that he guessed the truth when he found the Heming signature. His sudden, violent cry that he had "knocked up" the Shakespeare Papers may have been intended to surprise Samuel into an expression of self-betrayal, and when, for all his distress, Mr. Ireland showed no trace of a guilty conscience, Wallis may have turned his suspicion to the son. When William returned to Wallis with the new autographs, he would have been in a sufficiently nervous condition to break down under cross-examination and reveal his guilt in demeanour if not in actual words. If we assume that Wallis became convinced of the Papers' fabrication and took a sporting interest in helping their youthful forger to deceive the literary world, the rest of his behaviour becomes more comprehensible. His sudden conversion to ardent belief in place of an earlier hostility, his insistence on hearing the secret alone, and his attempt to maintain the Manuscripts when even their author denied them, may all have been part of the lawyer's eccentric delight in mocking and duping so many distinguished acquaintances. William may never have been sure that Wallis knew the truth; in any case, he would certainly have tried to avoid any suspicion of the other's complicity for fear of losing the credit for producing what he always regarded as works of genius. Whatever be the truth, the behaviour of Albany Wallis was certainly rather peculiar, and whatever his real motives he kept William's secret, and strengthened rather than shook Mr. Ireland's belief in the discoveries.

After the failure of *Vortigern* William began to lose control of his fancies, and the incipient paranoia that was already noticeable in the preceding winter at last found unrestrained expression. For eighteen months he had lived under continual pressure, working furtively at great speed whilst maintaining a pretence of his ordinary casualness, terrified by recurring fears of exposure, and exalted to extravagant conceit by the praises of the great and distinguished. Apart from the absent Talbot, William had no confidant, and even this tenuous partnership became more of an anxiety than an encouragement. Now the tension was relaxed, pretence was no longer possible and events lay beyond his control. Is it surprising that he let himself go?

At first William centred his fictions round the mysterious Gentleman, and through the agency of Mr. H., indulged all his day-dreams of grandeur and importance. The Gent., he told his father, was showing ever greater munificence, and had sent handsome gifts of money to Caulfield, Mrs. Powell and other actors who had done their best in the ill-fated *Vortigern*. To William himself he had redoubled his favours, lending him a curricle with horses and grooms, and promising him an estate of three hundred a year. The curricle actually existed, for early in May William took his sister Jane for a drive in it, but the expense of its upkeep was not sustained by any mysterious patron. "*The curricle horses*, he told us, about three weeks since, cost 100 guineas and were given him by the Gent.," wrote Mrs. Freeman, "but we find they *are* to cost 70, 50 of which have been paid by *him*, no other gent. having had anything to do in the business. He likewise had a curricle *building*, which was nearly finished, but Mr. Wallis kindly interfered and put a stop to its appearance." None of the family saw the estate, but William described it in considerable detail, saying that "there was an excellent old House on the Estate, and that the cellar was well stocked with good old port. The situation of the House was most beautiful, being near the sea and within 4 or 5 miles of his Friend's noble mansion." Mr. H. took his young *protégé* over his new domain, and after introducing him to his venerable steward entertained the pair to a lavish dinner at which "the old man chose Beef steaks and onions, which said onion sauce was serv'd in a Punch Bowl."

William soon grew tired of describing such distant wonders, and began to bring his fantasies nearer to the immediate interest of his audience. Soon after the production of *Vortigern* Samuel had shown *Henry II* to Mr. Harris of Covent Garden, who expressed much admiration for the love scenes, declaring them equal to anything he had ever read, and promised to present the play early in the following season. This was more than William's pride could withstand, and he made "strange speeches" to the family, saying that Harris had seen *William the Conqueror*,[1] considered it as good as *Henry II*, and was drawing up a contract by which William should provide him with two plays each season in return for £700 a year. As token of his goods intentions, the story added, Mr. Harris had promised to keep the curricle horses in his stable at Knightsbridge. When Samuel sought confirmation of his son's story, the manager seemed much surprised, and "inclined to think that his brain was affected."

About the beginning of May the family spent three days in the country, William riding a horse that he said belonged to the Gentleman, but which afterwards proved to have been hired for the occassion. At Shepperton, while dinner was preparing, he walked in the garden with Mrs. Freeman, and confided to her the secret of his forthcoming marriage. His future bride, said William, was named Miss Shaw, and lived with her wealthy family in Harley Street. She was "very handsome, about 17, and could not live without him"; and possessed, besides, an independent fortune of seven thousand pounds. Their first meeting had been highly romantic. Seeing William one night at the Opera, Miss Shaw had fallen in love with his melancholy beauty, and, after discovering his identity, contrived to meet him in Bond Street as if by chance. Mr. Shaw had at first forbidden the match, "but on the young lady having had a violent fit of illness on being foiled by her parents to see him, the intercession of her mother prevailed, and her father gave consent that he should visit at the House." "This story," observed

[1] William had enclosed a passage from this drama in one of the letters from Mr. H. (see Chapter VII). Apparently, the play was never completed.

Mrs. Freeman bitterly, "was delivered to me in the most solemn manner and with so many asservations with respect to the truth of it that even a Judge upon the Bench must have believed it."

Samuel was delighted by his son's splendid match, demanded an introduction to the lady's father, and discussed "what number of servants were necessary, what quantity of Linnen would be wanting, and whether £300 worth of Plate would be enough for first setting off." According to William, his father-in-law intended to provide him with an open carriage, while his wife was to have her mother's coach to return visits. Mr. H., who was an acquaintance of Mr. Shaw's, highly approved of the match, and promised partly to furnish a house for the young couple. For a time Samuel was well enough pleased, but as weeks passed without the appearance of Miss Shaw or word from her father, he began to make enquiries, and found, as he must have feared, that no one named Shaw had a house in Harley Street. Confronted with this, William changed the name to Shard, but although a family of that name did live in the street, they proved to have no daughter.

It is clear that William was losing his sense of proportion. The legend of Mr. H. had originally been invented to meet a definite need, and the later elaborations of the theme were largely an attempt to give more actuality to his rather nebulous munificence. The lies about Mr. Harris were of a different kind, being quite unnecessary and certain of rapid detection, while the elaborate invention of Miss Shaw could only have arisen from an advanced mental irresponsibility. For a time at least, William seems to have believed his own story, for he spread the news of the engagement among all his personal friends, and actually ordered "a very handsome bed and furniture." William liked to pose as a psychotic, and much of his flamboyant extravagance was undoubtedly due to conscious play-acting. At the same time he was genuinely neurotic in the real, and not the platitudinous, sense of the word, and by the beginning of May, 1796, the moody madness that had previously been largely a pose was coming dangerously near to reality. The conflict between his vanity, unnaturally inflamed by the events of the previous year, and the endless nagging reproaches of his father and family, shook him to the limit of his very uncertain stability. The situation was rapidly growing unendurable, and the path that William eventually chose was no doubt the only one left to him.

Inspired partly by vanity and partly by a genuine feeling of guilt, William repeatedly attempted to confess to his father that he was the sole forger of the Shakespeare Papers. But Samuel's contempt for his son's abilities, and his pathetically fierce conviction that fate could not so utterly have betrayed him, refused to let him admit what he must have known was the truth. For a time William tried to reveal that the Papers were forged without himself admitting the guilt of their fabrication. "Suppose," he suggested one morning at breakfast, "the Gent., to screen himself and family from any imputation of guilt in the business, should resolve on saying he *knew* them all to be forgeries?" But Samuel's reaction was not encouraging, and he replied violently "that it would, in his opinion, blast his character for ever, as it would appear a premeditated scheme to ruin an innocent family, in which he had made his own son the chief Instrument. Such a wretch, surely, does not exist."

Mrs. Freeman was more interested in the possibility, and on the following morning questioned William before his father came down:

> "I say'd to him that it was very generous in the Gent. to behave handsomely to the Performers, and asked him if he was to take the money to Mrs. Powell, to which he replied Yes. I then say'd that a man who could act in that manner would never have a thought of making the Papers appear forgeries—His reply was that he did not know that—What, I reply'd, can there be such a Wretch living that would join with a son and furnish him with the means of ruining his Father and whole Family—He say'd the Gent. might say he did not know it was a Forgery at first, but that afterwards he found Papers that let him into the business, and that was the reason he kept back what was promised to his father. My answer was that *the Parties who were to see him would no doubt insist on seeing those papers, which if he did not produce he could never again show his face, as it must appear such a complicated piece of Villainy,* but I would never believe such a Villain could exist on the face of the earth."

The continual allegations of his enemies began to break Samuel's spirit, and Mrs. Freeman takes an ever larger part in the management of his affairs. One evening late in May, after Mr. Ireland had retired, she cross-examined William in a last attempt to make him reveal the secret:

"Mr. Wallis means, I hope, to exculpate your father and us as from having any hand in this?"

"Certainly. It is for *that reason only* that the Party comes forward; he is drawing up something to be inserted in the Papers which, I suppose, will be shown to my father."

"Has Mr. Wallis seen the Gent.; because from the Paper

you gave me at Chambers you engaged that an interview should take place?"

"He has seen the Gent."

"What! I presume you mean yourself?"

"*No! The Gent.* He has conversed with him two or three times and will see him often, as he is giving Instructions for some Deed that is to be drawn up between them."

"I suppose nothing ill can attach to *him*, tho' it may to his Ancestor? Perhaps the Gent. possesses property that may have been unjustly come by."

"Oh! worse than that. If the matter were known it might render his character infamous; Mr. Wallis asserted that if it had been *his case* he would never on any terms have divulged the secret; but he is in every sense of the word a Gent. and a man of honour, and as such is most fit to be consulted, nor should the first Duke in the Kingdom know it; no, not anybody but himself."

"Does Mr. Wallis, from what he has heard, believe that the papers are genuine?"

"I presume he does, but is of the opinion that nothing more should be brought forward just at present."

"Do *you* believe they are genuine?"

"Most certainly I do."

"Have you any doubts respecting *any* of them?"

"I think the Deed of Gift to Ireland is informal."

"I have this afternoon been scrutinizing the papers very carefully, and, in my own mind, am convinced they must be genuine; and that *any Person* that was bold enough to say he did them would only render himself infamous; for though the business might appear ingenious, it would likewise appear a *dreadful Imposition,* and not even a share of merit would accrue to him till after he was dead."

"You are right, that is always the case with works of Genius."

"There are many odd circumstances by which valuable discoveries might no doubt be made; for instance now, don't you remember about two or three years ago, an old Gent. was murdered, I believe in Clifford's Inn; now such a man might have been possessed of valuable papers."

"I don't recollect anything about such a circumstance, but if the papers were taken away, those papers might have been sold, and if the person who purchas'd them knew that they had been stolen, the buyer would be equally culpable with the thief; but if a lawyer were consulted even in a case of murder he could not disclose the business, for by his profession he is sworn to secrecy on the part of his client."

"Did you not tell me that the Play which you took to Mr. Harris was, he said, *finer* than the Henry?"

"*No,* he did not say finer, but quite as fine."

"Your father, and all of us, have reason to be offended at not having seen the Play before you took it to Mr. Harris."

"I should have shown it, but that he is always for cutting out and making alterations. Mr. Harris wants me to introduce a new scene, and let Rosamund be poison'd on the stage."

"Do you intend doing it?"

"Perhaps I may."

"If Talbot and you were to die, I think you have often said the whole secret must be known?"

"I don't say that: the World have got hold of a wrong

notion about Talbot; he is no more concerned in the business than either *you* or my *sister*."

"Why, did he not give you the first paper; he said himself he did?"

"That is another thing. I don't say anything about that.

"I think your father or Mr. Wallis ought to see the things mentioned in the schedule, but particularly the miniature picture, and your father, I am sure, would enter into any agreement not to shew or make any use of them."

"Mr. Wallis will determine that. . . ."

It was after midnight before William got to his bed. He must have realised that he had committed himself too far and that pretence was running out.

Mrs. Freeman saw with equal clarity that the situation had become impossible, and expressed her fears in a vigorous letter to Talbot:

"When I resolve on a passage in your letter, my nature shudders at the mysterious business, and I cannot help pitying the situation both of *yourself* and Sam. Your words are: that you hope the offer of making the Affidavit will be accepted definitely without urging any more Proposals, since any others must of necessity be declined by you, though your *Life* were the forfeit for being secret. After such a Declaration can I then suppose that *Sam*, who is equally involved with yourself, had ever any intention of mentioning the *real truth* either to Mr. Wallis or any other person? No, it is impossible, *he* could no more than you betray his trust; but much I fear that to quiet (as he may think) the Public Mind he has invented some story that will involve the mystery still deeper, and my opinion is strengthened by a determined resolution he has formed to quit the Kingdom *immediately*, though he says that of late he has been inspired with all the

Furor of a Divine Poet. Such is the pityable situation in which we are likely to be left, nor does *he* seem to feel a grain of remorse on the occasion, but has deserted his office (for a genius like his, he says, cannot condescend to sit at a desk) and does nothing but lounge about the streets, or drive about either on Horseback, or in a curricle with a groom after him like a Man of the first Fashion. . . ."

At the end of May Samuel went down to Sunning for a much needed holiday, and on Sunday, June 5th, wrote a plain and touching appeal to his son:

"It is now more than a week, my dear Sam, since I left London, and not a word or a line from you. In the situation, unsettled as you are, you cannot suppose but that my mind is much agitated both on your account and that of your family. I expected, according to your promise, that you would certainly have written to me and have pointed out what was your plan, and not only so but your intention with regard to the papers. I do assure you my state is truly wretched on both acounts. I have no rest either night or day, which might be much alleviated by a more open and candid Conduct on your side. Surely if there is a person for whom you can for a moment feel, it must be for a Parent who has never ceased to render you every comfort and attention, from your earliest moment of existence to the present. I think you must sometimes reflect and place yourself in your imagination as at a future period of life, having a son and being in such a predicament as I stand at the moment; and then judging what must be *your state of mind,* and what must be *mine at present.* I do not mean reproaches by this letter, but to assure you that if you cannot think me your friend, I fear you will be deceived in all friendships that you may in future form. I do not recollect that any conduct of mine towards you has been other than that of a friend and companion—not that of a rigid or morose Parent. It is therefore surely doubly unnatural that I should be forced to apply for Information of any kind when I ought to hear it voluntarily from yourself. You seem to be estranging yourself not only from me but from all your family and all my acquaintance. Reflect well what you do and what determination you make, for this is the moment that may in all probability render you comfortable in your Establishment and future Situation, or make you an alien to happiness for ever. I have heard much of my situation with the World as to the papers at Reading, from many Gentlemen there, who all agree that my state is truly a pitiable one, and all seem to dread the event. I know not the nature of your oaths and engagements, nor does the World; but it is universally allowed that no obligation should lead a parent into ruin. If the papers are to be established as genuine why delay to furnish me with those documents so long promised? But I will say no more on the subject at the present. . . . Remember me kindly to all, and believe me, whatever may be your future Destiny, your very sincere Friend and affectionate Father."

But William never received the letter, for on the Monday morning, before the post arrived, he had taken the only possible decision.

On Tuesday the 7th, Jane Ireland wrote to her father.

"I hope, my dearest father, you do not consider it as inattention my not having written to you, as I really considered it an unnecessary expense when my aunt so fully gave every detail of the circumstances that occurred from day to day in her letters.

"I went on Saturday evening (to stay till Monday) at Lambeth; Anne and Robert[1] having pressed me much to pass

[1] Samuel's elder daughter and her husband, Robert Barnard.

a day with them. My aunt came to dinner on Sunday and we returned together last evening, but have not seen or heard anything of Sam, except indeed from the Maid, who rather alarmed us about him. She said he had been talking a great deal about going away, and said he was to receive £50 yesterday morning, and told her he meant to make *her a present*, as soon as he had it in his power. She asked him for his linen that was to be sent to the *Wash*, his answer was, 'no! I shall take it all away as it is, and pack it up at the *Gentleman's* I am going to, as there are new Trunks for me there,' and that he should return the Boxes he took away as they were merely temporary conveniences. She said he was very busy in the early part of the morning tying up his clothes, and when he had completed that, the boy was desired to call him a Coach, and he put the things in, desiring the man to *follow him* (avoiding by that means telling the Coachman where he was to drive to before the servants). He left word with the Maid, he should be in again in the evening, but he did not return nor have we seen anything of him to-day."

William never did return. His dramatic departure was final.

Chapter Fifteen

CONFESSION

From the time he left home, William's movements become increasingly difficult to trace. On June 4th, the Saturday before his departure, he was married at Clerkenwell Church to a Miss Alice Crudge, and the "shortish woman who appeared to be a girl of the town and not very handsome," with whom he was seen on Sundays in Kennington Gardens, was probably his wife. We hear also of him riding on horseback with a servant behind him, showing himself nightly at the play, and sitting in a coffee house in deep conversation with a distinguished elderly gentleman. William kept in touch with Albany Wallis and became increasingly friendly with Byng, but he neither visited his father nor gave him his address. On June 14th he wrote Samuel a defiant letter of apology:

"If, my dear father (for so I must still call you) there remains any particle of that love and affection for me which has always been proud to show itself, you will not, I am sure, destroy this before you have perused it. Do not conceive I mean to clear myself of the rashness I have been guilty of but only to say a few words which will tend greatly to soften the anguish of my mind, and perhaps ameliorate the wretchedness of your feelings. That I have written the Papers I confess; You, I believe, are also convinced by what Mr. B. produced when you were at his house, but for the language you think *me* incapable, and there it is I am wrong'd. Can you think so meanly of me as to be the *Tool* of some person of Genius? No Sir I scorn the thought; were it not that I am *Author* as well as Writer I would have died rather than confess it. The Vortigern I wrote; if I copied anyone it was the Bard himself, in no one paper, book or parchment was I furnished with language by any one living—if there is Soul or Imagery it is *my own*. The Henry II was more mine than the Vortigern, as I scarce look'd into any one Book while I wrote it. . . . I beg your acceptance of the publication of Vortigern and the whole of the profits of Henry II. Should I live, my future labours shall equally be devoted to the good of my family. Do not wish to meet me, my dear father, I cannot yet bear it. I will instantly retire into Wales and give myself up to that study I so ardently wish for.

If the writer of the Papers, I mean the mind that breathes through them, shows any spark of Genius and deserves Honour, *I, Sir, your son,* am that person, and if I live but for a little I will prove it. Mr. Talbot knew only the secret . . . nor he nor any one living had any concern in either writing or composing save myself alone, and to that I pledge my every hope of happiness. If I speak false, may the Almighty judge me accordingly. . . ."

Samuel's reply was hard and bitter:

"Let your talent be what it may—who do you think will ever sanction you, or associate with you after showing an ability for such gross and deliberate impositions on the public, and through the medium of your own father. Impositions of such a nature to the well-being of society that the Law holds out certain death as a reward first when detected. The subject is too horrid for reflection, I shall leave you to your own thoughts on the occasion. . . . I find you have parted with all your books, tho' you sacredly promised me but a few days before I left Town, that a few of them shd. be reserv'd for me if I chose to purchase them; and what is worse, I find that the money they have provided is dissipated, and your debts all unpaid, although so fully conscious as you must be of my inability to discharge them! I have not words to express the high indignation I feel at yr. unnatural Conduct—words or reproaches are now all vain. You have left me with a load of misery and have, I fear, about you a load of infamy that you will find perhaps more difficulty than I shall in getting rid of."

For an instant Samuel seems to admit that his son is indeed the forger of the Shakespeare Papers. In the moment of clarity that showed him the truth he also realised the crude necessity of maintaining the pretence, and in a second letter practically ordered his son to continue an acknowledged deception.

"In my letter of yesterday I forgot to hint to you the dangerous predicament you stand in if you are, as you say, the writer etc. of these deeds. Your character, if you insist on this, will be blasted, that no person will admit you into their house, nor can you anywhere be trusted. Therefore, do not suffer yourself from vanity or any other motive to adhere to any such confession."

To this suggestion, if suggestion it was, of persistence in an admitted fraud, William returned a decisive refusal. "I will immediately set about writing a pamphlet," he replied, "wherein I will explain the business. If the world should spurn me," he concluded ominously, "I know what course to take."

From that time forward the split between father and son was complete, and Samuel maintained the authenticity of the Papers without weakening or restraint. Byng, who had grown fond of the young forger, tried to convince Mr. Ireland that William had confessed the truth, and showed him as evidence forgeries and poems that had actually been composed in his presence. But Samuel refused to hear argument, and in anger at these attempts to destroy the belief that now preoccupied his whole life, rejected his friend's endeavours to bring about a reconciliation. "Your young man is a prodigy one way or other," Byng wrote from the country, "and to cover one Deceit has told a thousand Lies. But they have begat each other, and were not intended at starting.

"I come to this place to shelter from my family; and wish sometimes to change a son and run the risk of Genius. . . . Allow me to say, if he is to be saved—it must not be by harshness, as his mind always seems to *harden* when that is used towards him. However he may deserve it—you ought to know [best] but I only judge from what I have seen. He seems quite affected whenever he thinks of you as his Parent. Feel kindly towards him. . . ."

Byng's advice was useless. How could Mr. Ireland feel kindly towards a son who by his former deceit and his present confession seemed determined to drive him to ruin? Ignoring his son's protestations of guilt, Samuel sought every means to re-establish his own credit and that of the Manuscripts. In June he published a declaration of innocence, in the *True Briton*, but no one believed him; and once again he turned his hopes to Montague Talbot, repeatedly imploring him to reveal the truth, or at least make an unqualified statement as to the genuineness of the Discoveries. But Talbot was firm in his refusal to go any further than his original suggestion of a joint affidavit, and reasserted his unshakable loyalty to the promises he claimed to have sworn. Mrs. Freeman suspected that he was loyal to William rather than to a mysterious gentleman, and sent him an emotional denunciation of his unworthy friend:

". . . Since not any of his friends have ever discovered the least trait of *literary genius* in his character, he circulates a

report that *He* alone is the author of the papers and the plays
of Vortigern and Henry II, the former is a very good one, the
latter most excellent; but I who know his talent for romanc-
ing so well can never credit the report. When I reflect on his
conduct towards his father in the whole business, the
atrocity of the Act is unparalleled in history. He, poor man,
is sunk almost to despair, and is of all Beings the most
pitiable, for 'it is not an open Enemy that has done him this
dishonour, *since then* (in the language of the Scripture) he
might have borne it,' but it is even his *child*, his *companion*.
He (wretched outcast) who ought to have been his *Faithful
Friend*. Oh! Sir, reflect I say but on the atrocity of the act, and
then think if any punishment can be devised adequate to the
enormity of the crime, a crime that involves his whole family
in *Ruin*."

But Talbot remained unmoved, and to further attempts to
turn him against William merely replied: "I cannot help
wondering at his silence to me, but whenever I may chance to
meet him, I shall be proud to own him as a friend."

Samuel was not long content with such mild methods of
persuasion, and in the middle of the summer hinted that unless
Talbot told the truth about the Papers, he would use his
influence with the Lord-Lieutenant of Ireland to have him dismissed from his Dublin theatre. Talbot was dismayed and
furious at the threat, and replied with anxious violence that
Samuel had no influence with the Lord-Lieutenant, and that if
he had, the Lord-Lieutenant would refuse to put pressure on
the Theatre, and that if he did, the Management would refuse to
be coerced, and that if they were, it didn't matter anyway.
"You know though I am not a Man of Fortune I am not dependent on the stage for a livelihood, and that if I was so dependent

a situation might be easily obtained elsewhere. I have for some time talked of embarking for America, and I have not yet determined to forego these Intentions. . . ." But in spite of his brave words, Talbot was sufficiently alarmed to offer an affidavit of his belief in Samuel's innocence, on condition that he was asked to play no further part in the controversy.

Meanwhile, William was in no better case than his father. He had even succeeded in further injuring both their interests by alienating Mr. Harris of Covent Garden; for when Samuel met the Manager at Wallis's house, he found him rather cooler about the merits of *Henry II*, and discovered that William "had been spouting some speeches to Mr. H. as a specimen of his talent as an orator." In July or August William went to Wales with Albany Wallis, but as Byng rather gleefully told Mr. Ireland, the venture was not a success:

> "Mrs. B. is with me; and has received a long History from Mr. W—— of your stray son;—in which tho' much oddity and wildness of temper may be atributed to him, there appears to be nothing very improper or reproachable.
> From the vehemence of Mr. W's Temper, the difficulty in settling in that country, and after many wild and inconceivable Histories, he determined upon going to Devonshire to his *friend at Tiverton* (*remember all that*; and who is He?); and accordingly by the kind assistance of Mrs. W., who advanced him *five guineas* out of her own pocket (which you must instantly repay me) he took his second flight, by the way of *todler-conveyance* to Gloucester."[1]

[1] There does seem to have been a friend at Tiverton, for one of William's letters is postmarked from that place. But his mysterious references to the immense wealth of the man lead one to suspect that he may have been another Mr. H.

Whoever his friends may have been, William did not go to Tiverton. An acquaintance of Samuel's wrote that a friend of his had "lately met with a young man in Gloucester travelling on foot in Trowsers by the name of Ireland. He said he was intimately acquainted with Mr. Byng, that he had been in the 81st Regt.—and professed a violent love for antiquity, and when an old book was spoken of, expressed a most eager wish to see it, and have it, if *Money* could procure it—yet I understand that coin of the present reign was to the young Antiquary as precious as old gold, and that he was glad to borrow a few bright guineas. He was described as very sprightly and very dashing—a spouting Richard, one who would have been a choice companion for young Harry & Co. and well suited in these days for certain folks of like disposition. Now who would believe that so young a man and such a young man could have found leisure even barely to transcribe the Papers. . . ." It must have been a curious meeting—the long-haired, handsome young man, still dashing and voluble in spite of his poverty and his trowsers whitened with summer dust, and the middle-aged, superior gentleman fresh from his post-chaise. There is something almost heroic in William's imaginative self-assurance.

By the beginning of September, William had found a temporary resting-place, and writes to Byng in an easy, natural style, free, for the first time in months, from rhetoric or hysteria:

"At length, my Dr. Sir, I think I have a situation which is at once perfectly retired as well as Romantick. I am within a few miles of the finest spot in the Kingdom, which over looks all the Bristol Channel, the Sea, and the Welsh Mountains. . . . I look in the papers now and then, and I am happy to find the business of the MSS. is totally dropp'd. I hope my father will be better convinced; if he is not I fear there will be more pride in his *mind* than *real candid judgment.* I will again beg of you to speak to my Father and Mr. Franklyn about me. Mr. F. offered me £30 for the first year. I am now pretty well settled, but have no money unless permitted to draw immediately. . . . I have a most excellent story, mostly formed by myself[1] which I am convinced will have good effect at representation. I shall introduce songs, etc., castles, etc., wonders, etc., as you hinted. . . ."

The days at Bristol passed very happily. William seems to have written little—with him creation was best inspired by neurosis—but spent the time idling, walking and seeing the sights of the neighbourhood. His first thought, of course, was to visit Chatterton's birthplace and inspect the tower where he claimed to have found the Rowley Poems. After this pilgrimage William called on Mrs. Newton, the dead poet's sister, in search of fresh anecdotes of his youthful life and genius. Mrs. Newton had very little new to say, but the old stories of the wonderful youth's blazing eye, zest for learning, and moody stoicism seemed specially vivid from the lips of one who had actually known them.

William's happy seclusion was not untroubled for long. The five guineas he had borrowed from Mrs. Wallis were soon exhausted, and one of his numerous creditors, a Mr. Jones of Golden Square, discovered his new address. "The worst that can befall me," wrote William despondently, "is Gaol, and I am reconciled to my fate . . . is the *Piano-Forte* lost?, for I could

[1] Albany Wallis had supplied William with a plot that he suggested should be written up into a story. This may have been the inspiration of *The Abbess.*

raise then £20 to liquidate that demand, and thus cancel my greatest creditor by returning the Property. . . ." In his desperate want of money he imposed on one of Samuel's friends who lived in the district, and obtained a loan by pretending he was helping his father to gather material for an intended book. But such shifts could not support him for long, and in the late autumn he returned to London.

William may have imagined that interest in the Forgeries was "totally dropp'd," but his father still felt the effects on his own reputation, and found that the charges now commonly made against him both tarnished his honour and affected his means of livelihood. Even those who bore no personal malice and only half believed in Mr. Ireland's guilt, had a natural disinclination to purchase prints and antiques from a man who might well have manufactured them in another part of his premises; while the professional journalists who earned a precarious livelihood by slandering the hated and helpless, continued to find the Ireland Manuscripts a fruitful source of scurrility when nothing more up-to-date presented itself. Harried by the Press and suspected by his customers, Samuel set to work on a pamphlet that should clear his own repute and destroy that of Edmund Malone. The decision was probably unwise, and, as his friends suggested, more likely to revive the slowly dying controversy than silence the enemies of the Papers, but Mr. Ireland was now too distraught to listen to reason, and persisted in his determination.

William was deeply disturbed when he heard of his father's decision. At the best, a reaffirmation of the Papers' authenticity would prejudice his own admittance of authorship; at the worst it might stigmatise him as the basest sort of perjurer. He resolved to counteract such a disaster by issuing his own confession in a printed pamphlet, and asked the assistance of Albany Wallis. On this occasion too, Wallis behaved rather strangely, and attempted to dissuade William from making his confession public. As a last resort, presumably, he told Samuel that William "was in great distress, that he was a very great Genius, and was going to publish a pamphlet in a few days in which he would avow himself the Author of all the Papers"; and arranged a meeting between father and son.

On December 12th Samuel saw William at Wallis's house. "He met me in the room with much coldness and indifference," noted Mr. Ireland, "and said he was the author of the papers . . . he said he was in great want of money and must publish it to get money. I asked him who wrote his pamphlet. He said *himself*. I then turned to Mr. Wallis (whom I begged not to quit the room) and observed that if he was the Author and no one was called in to correct it, that it would be so ill-written, he would give himself the lie in all he said, and that no one would believe the author of it could be the author of the Papers—to which Mr. Wallis assented, and said he had just told him so, and in proof of it that he had himself expunged a great many passages that were so bad as to render it too much so to be read, and in any degree to be credited. He still persisted, however, in publishing the pamphlet, and said he and his printer would correct it and render it fit for the Public Eye. . . . Fully dissatisfied we parted." The next day William wrote his father a violent and insulting letter:

Decr. 13. 1796.

". . . As I am in want of Money as I told you yesterday I should thank you to send by Mr. Scott my [?] and Prints Illustrative, as by the sale of it I shall be enabled to discharge some small Debts and also keep *Myself* from immediate *Want*—In a few days I should wish also to have my *Armour, small book case, Press* and *Desk* when I shall also sell them and pay my Debts, according to the Sum they yield. . . ."

William signed his name with a flourish and paused for a moment. Then, with the angry frustration of years behind him, he scrawled his signature into "W. H. Freeman." With the letter he enclosed fragments of parchment browned with age and signed, in Elizabethan handwriting, Shakespeare, Elizabeth, Southampton and W. H. Freeman. The break with his father was complete.

A few days later, he published *An Authentic Account of the Shakespearian Manuscript,* in which he fully and plainly confessed his authorship of the Forgeries. "In justice to the world," began the Preface, "and to remove the odium under which my father labours by publishing the manuscripts brought forward by me as *Shakespeare's,* I think it necessary to give a true account of the business, hoping that whatever may occur in the following pages will meet with favour and forgiveness, when considered as the act of a boy." The printer must have been an efficient sub-editor, for the pamphlet reads without either bombast or turgidity; but, as Samuel had prophesied, both believers and enemies received it with complete incredulity. When the *True Briton* remarked that the account did not contain "a single spark of genius, talent or taste, nor the smallest portion of that *feeling* which certainly appears in various parts of the MSS.," it expressed the common opinion, and the confession was generally considered a product of William's vanity or his father's cowardliness.

In the same month appeared *Mr. Ireland's Vindication of his*

Conduct respecting the Publication of the supposed Shakespeare MSS.
The Vindication is a helpless and pathetic document. Samuel
gives the two Certificates of Belief and all their signatories,
quotes a censored version of Montague Talbot's account of the
discovery of the Papers, and bitterly attacks Malone's personal
character and scholastic abilities. But, like his son, Samuel
was given no credit, and the two pamphlets were bought,
discussed, and wholly disbelieved.

William had apparently expected that the disclosure of his
part in the Forgeries would bring him immediate literary
recognition, and the failure of the *Authentic Account* made him
aware of his unpleasantly precarious prospects. At the beginning of January, 1797, he abandoned pride and wrote again to
his father:

"Jany. 3 1797.

Dr. Sir,

As various opinions seem to agitate the public mind since
my publishing the *Authentic Account* of the *MSS* given by
myself to you, which would tend to frustrate any attempt
I might make of appearing on the stage, and not knowing
what step it is most expedient that I could take as to my
future welfare—I apply Sir to you *not* for *pecuniary aid,* but
advice and perhaps assistance of another kind—

If you are *really* my father, I appeal to your feelings as a
Parent, if not, I am the more indebted to you for the Care
of my youthful Education etc. and though I cannot expect
so much, yet I shall hope from you that degree of feeling due
to every Man from a Fellow Creature—I have said *if* you
are my parent, being at a loss to account for the expressions
so often us'd to Mrs. Freeman, and which she has repeatedly
told me of 'that you did not think me *your son,*' besides, after
slight altercations with Mrs. F. you have frequently said

that when of age you have a story to tell me that would astonish and (if I mistake not) much shock me. Mrs. F. after my bringing forward the Papers us'd ironically to say 'that now you was glad enough to own me for your son.' If, my dear Sir, you know anything relating to myself, I intreat you to inform me of it. But should it be merely a story appertaining to my *mother* which might give me pain, I trust you will bury it in oblivion, nay, I am sure you will, for Delicacy, I am convinced, is no stranger to your Bosom.

That I have been guilty of a fault in giving you the MSS I *confess* and am sorry for it, but I must also assure you it was without a bad intention or a thought of what would ensue. As you have repeatedly said, '*Truth will find its Basis,*' so will your *Character* (notwithstanding all aspersions) shortly appear unblemish'd to the world. To the above Expression *I* also appeal, and though any Pamphlet, compar'd with *my* Vortigern and *my* Henry II etc. etc. may for the present convince the world that I am not *author* of them, yet, Sir, I may sacredly appeal to my *God*, that Time which develops Truth will authenticate the contents of *my Pamphlet* and thereby '*Never Erring Truth Find Its Basis.*' I am exceedingly sorry you did not (before the Publication of your Book) inspect the Papers in Mr. Wallis's possession (and which I understand you might have seen), as they contain no other than a similar account to that already publish'd by me. I make this remark, as it still throws a *Mystery* on the Business, and will give the world an idea of some conceal'd account being divulg'd by *me* to Mr. Wallis.

But the principal purport of this Letter is to inform you of my wish of getting into some Situation and way of life which may keep me from *Starving.* I use this Expression as it will soon come to this Crisis—you, Sir, have many acquaintances that might aid me in getting some situation, for I care not what it is so I can but depend on it. The

Money[1] which I have receiv'd for my Pamphlet, I have been living upon, and that must soon be quite exhausted; as to writing
for the stage, I can do that at my leisure Hours but can
place no *certain* dependence on it—If any person would give
me a situation which required *money down* I would write for
them till something succeeded which might repay them the
sum required. If you will mention this among your various
friends who may have it in their power, you will save me
not only from *Want* but also from *Despair*. . . ."

If Samuel revealed the family secret, we have no record of it,
and through the following months he and his son squabbled
over the latter's debts and the sale of such of his property as
still remained at Norfolk Street. But he appears to have been
moved by William's evident want, and at the end of March
arranged a meeting in the house of Albany Wallis. By this time
William's pride was roused, and, when he saw his father, he
stood upon his dignity. "He addressed me in a very cool
insulting manner," noted Samuel, "neither touched his hat
nor offered his hand—not did he even express any contrition
for what had passed. I told him I neither did nor ever would
believe him to be the author of the Papers—till he gave specimens of his abilities equal to what I had in my possession. He
had the audacity to say 'he could not write for he had no
money' . . . he again and again asserted boldly that he was the
author of the whole. I then called for proofs without which
neither the world nor myself wd. credit him. He said he cared
not for the world and as for myself he was sure I would not
believe him the author. . . . I replied that I believed he neither
could nor *would* be able to bring proofs that would convince the

---

[1] Apparently £10.

public. He said impudently: 'those are *bold* and *hard* words for any man to *dare* to say!' on which I observed I was not accustomed to such language and withdrew downstairs." Mr. Ireland and his son never met again.

Chapter Sixteen

ANTICLIMAX

Samuel's position grew steadily worse, and his confidence and health began to break up under the continual allegations that were made against him. In 1797 Gillray engraved a caricature bearing a particularly vicious inscription, and Samuel took counsel's opinion on the prospects of an action for libel. "The title of the print," he wrote to his lawyer, Mr. Tidd, "is 'Notorious Characters, No. I,' with the following remark, 'Mr. Bromley in his Catalogue, etc., p. 390 has erroneously put this portrait into his *seventh* class—it ought to have appeared in the *tenth*—see the Contents of it, p. 449.' On reference to the page in Mr. Bromley's book, it seems the class alluded to is that of 'Convicts and persons otherwise remarkable' . . ." Mr. Tidd's reply was not encouraging. There was, he said, a perfectly obvious libel, but since the defendants would plead justification, Mr. Ireland's case would depend on the evidence of his son. And Mr. Tidd did not think that William would make a good impression in a Court of Law. Samuel sought other advice, and actually started proceedings, but no one offered support, and he finally let the matter drop. As this and similar libels went unchecked, business at Norfolk Street came almost to a standstill, and the sales of his latest book, *Picturesque Views on the River Wye*, were practically negligible. Constitutional disorders troubled a body worn out by anxiety, and Samuel suffered severely from diabetes. But even his own illness scarcely aroused his attention.[1]

[1] His doctor ordered him to note the quantity of water he made daily, but Samuel dropped the record after three days.

William's condition was equally unhappy. In December he wrote to his father and begged for money, confessing that he had pawned his plate and was living on the sale of his wife's personal effects. He was still proud, in spite of his difficulties, and concluded his letter with an underlined plea for secrecy:

> "I request that you will destroy this letter nor ever mention a syllable of its contents for it is enough to know oneself poor without enjoying either the world's facetious pity, or cool contempt."

But Samuel, embittered by Gillray's cartoon and the poor prospects of his lawsuit, not only refused the request, but spitefully made the letter public. He apparently encouraged rumours against the character of his son's wife, for William ingenuously complains that "although Mrs. Ireland is lawfully my wife, and has for sixteen months past conducted herself in the most irreproachable manner, calumny has not spared her, but branded her with the title of my mistress." In 1798 William borrowed money from his wife, and with 1,200 novels started a circulating library in Princes Place, Kennington. He had obtained the books partly on credit, and for the last time sought his father's help: "The person with whom I have contracted for the Novels would willingly take a few of your works in Payment. If, therefore, you could render me such a service, believe me, sir, I shall regard it as a debt, and should success favour my wishes, will faithfully pay you."[1] Samuel did not reply. William seems never to have written to his father again.

---

[1] William asked for ten volumes. There must still have been a considerable demand of Samuel's works, if so small a number was worth any great proportion of twelve hundred novels.

"Such cursed assurance,"
"Is past all endurance." *Maid of the Mill.*

"*The Fourth Forger*"

From a cartoon by Gillray after a self-portrait by Samuel Ireland

The *Authentic Account* had taken the heart from the controversy, but discussion dragged on to the end of the century. In
1797 George Chalmers, the antiquarian, published his *Apology
for the Believers in the Shakespeare Papers,* in which, without maintaining their authenticity, he attacked Malone with as much
discursive venom as the latter had shown in his *Inquiry.*
Chalmers enjoyed controversy, for when his enemy failed to
make a reply, he published a *Supplemental Apology* in which he
repeated and expanded his earlier arguments. Though Malone
was silent, others were ready to answer, and for a time the
dispute recovered a flicker of vitality. But the Forgeries were
almost a dead issue, and it is symbolic enough that Chalmers'
grandly entitled *Appendix to a Supplemental Apology for the
Believers* should discuss the authorship of the Letters of Junius.

Samuel himself continued his lonely campaign for belief in
the Papers, and supported his faith with the hope that there
would "in all probability be atonement at the death of the
original proprietor." Mr. Harris, in spite of his early enthusiasm, had refused to produce *Henry II* on the ground that it
was too unpolished, and Samuel sought the professional help of
Arthur Murphy, the dramatist, to doctor the play into commercial success. He had suggested an equal division of profits as
a fair reward for rewriting, but Murphy, with tactful firmness,
preferred a more certain remuneration:

"When I consider that there is in the play, as it stands,
a great deal of very good matter, which wants nothing from
me but proper arrangement, I cannot think of taking an
equal share of the profits: that would be beyond all the bounds
of Reason. A successful play may be worth 6 or 700 £,
perhaps more; what claim can I have to one half? I will tell

you what has occurred to me: I suppose the alterations will take at least two months of my time: in weighing the compensation for that, I have gone as high as I think becomes me, and also as low as I think I ought, and the result is that I am willing to undertake the business for 150£, without having any further claim of any kind."

Samuel replied with an equally tactful repetition of his original offer, but Murphy refused to be moved, and the matter was dropped.

Unless the Manuscripts could be proved genuine, there was no hope of their winning success, and in 1797 Samuel published *An Investigation Into Mr. Malone's Claim to the Character of a Scholar or Critic*, in which he vented all his futile anger against his victorious antagonist. "I felt I had a right," he declares, "to expose the incompetency of Mr. Malone as a man of learning, upon the only subject which he affects to know; and I more strongly felt it a duty to expose his unworthy and disingenuous conduct as a Man." The pamphlet succeeds in discrediting a few of the critic's more dogmatic pronouncements, but the Shakespeare Papers were hastening to an oblivion from which no quibble or slander could hope to resurrect them. In 1799 Samuel published *Vortigern* and *Henry II*, with introductions in which he avowed his innocence of forgery, attacked Malone, Kemble and Phillimore, and proclaimed his complete estrangement from William, "the cause of all this public and domestic misfortune." The plays had a very small sale, mostly being purchased as trophies by the opponents of the Discoveries.

In July 1800 Samuel died, declaring almost on his death-bed "that he was totally ignorant of the deceit, and was equally a believer in the authenticity of the manuscripts as those which were even the most credulous." When his books and curiosities were sold by auction, Edmund Malone bid up to 120 guineas for the Shakespeare Papers.

William Ireland lived to be sixty, but he never fulfilled his apparent early promise. For some time after the final estrangement from his father, he kept himself alive by copying out forgeries in the old hand and selling them to collectors of curiosa; and friends of his family who believed he was too harshly treated by society, charitably engaged him to inlay copies of his own confession or Samuel's *Vindication* and extra-illustrate them with specimens of the forged documents, until rumours of his dishonesty put a stop to this kind of employment. Unable to obtain regular work, William sank into the precarious routine of the literary hack. His first novel, *The Abbess* was published before the end of the century, and for the remaining thirty years of his life he ground out novels, satires, squibs, plays and histories under a variety of pseudonyms. Few of his works met with any great success; and although all of them show some literary talent, they want the imagination that, for all their crudity, distinguished the Shakespeare Papers.

In more than one respect the Forgeries ruined William's career. Far from forgiving the deception as "the impetuous act of a boy," the literary public were especially enraged by the youth and inexperience of their deceiver. Sir Isaac Heard, Dr. Parr, George Chalmers and others of the learned believers could have borne to be duped by a scholar or experienced writer, but to have worshipped the scribblings of a boy scarce able to punctuate was an indignity that neither they nor their enemies ever forgot. Without showing open vindictiveness, they were permanently hostile to William, preventing the performance of his plays and successfully deriding his poetry. The principal protagonists always remembered the controversy, and never changed their attitude towards the author of their delusion.

A quarter of a century later William met James Boaden, now a distinguished literary man, the biographer of Mrs. Siddons and Kemble, and an acknowledged Shakespearian authority, at a publisher's in Bond Street. The pair strolled together, talking, inevitably, of Shakespeare and the long-dead fabrications. At the corner of Buckingham Street, Boaden paused and gave his final judgment on the Ireland Forgeries. "You must be aware, sir," he said, "of the enormous crime you committed against the divinity of Shakespeare. Why, the act, sir, was nothing short of sacrilege; it was precisely the same thing as taking the holy Chalice from the altar and * * * * * * * therein!!!" "To hear an aged, walking mass of mortality," comments William, "utter such a sample of mingled pedantry and folly, has left such an indelible impression upon my mind, that I never pass the spot in question, without a sentiment of pity, on recalling the ravings of a self-created expounder of Shakespeare, dwindled into second childhood." If the world never forgave the forger, William never forgot his persecutors.

The early acceptance of the Forgeries did at least as much as their subsequent exposure to stifle and inhibit William's talents. The contrast between the hysterical rapture with which the Papers were first received, and the equally hysterical condemnation amidst which they were finally buried, was sufficiently striking to indicate that one of the judgments was based wholly on emotional prejudice. Looking on the matter from William's viewpoint, it might well be argued that whereas the

228

original praise was purely spontaneous, dictated neither by personal interest nor self-protection, the later contempt was clearly in part a revenge for having been so publicly deceived, and in part a violent reaction against a violent passion. Judged purely by itself, without reference to its actual object, the early admiration was more likely to be genuine than the subsequent animosity. If you believed, as William did, that the Papers were at least highly talented, there was every excuse for anger and stubborn embitterment.

William thought himself hardly treated, and the memory of the Forgeries, instead of dying away to a lurid reminiscence, remained an ever-present influence throughout his life. The style of writing that had ravished the critics almost to tears must have elements of greatness, and persistence in the course he had begun would bring, William believed, the posthumous glory of a Chatterton. And so, in most of his serious works, he retained the manner and feeling of his first endeavours, and condemned himself to an endless imitation of his own immature fabrications.

In spite of their clumsiness, the forged plays show a considerable degree of ability and dramatic feeling. A boy of nineteen who could write such lines as:

> "*Give me another sword, I have so clogg'd*
> *And budged this with blood, and slipp'ry gore,*
> *That it does mock my gripe. A sword, I say . . .*"

or:

> "*Then waving thrice his casèd hand in air*
> *And with a nod that spread pale fear around*
> *And seem'd to animate his bloody plume,*
> *Triumphantly he bade them all defiance.*"

shows great promise, if nothing more; and the fashionable contempt for the Forgeries was as unjustified as William's later work was disappointing. Whatever may have been his poetic potentialities, William possessed theatrical gifts of a high order, and even the unfortunate *Vortigern* is well constructed, with effective transition of action and vigorous development of plot. But the theatre was closed to the forger who had once deceived it, and *Mutius Scævola*, a blank-verse drama which William wrote in 1801, was rejected with contempt by the managements that presented other far inferior plays.

William's later years had their adventures and adversities, but he never recaptured his youthful notoriety. In the intervals of his hackwork he produced a Frogmore Fête for Princess Alice, was imprisoned for debt, spent many years in France, and married a second time, having one daughter. He outlived most of those connected with the controversy. Edmund Malone died in 1812, after making a complete collection of the pamphlets relating to the forgeries, and Dr. Parr followed him in 1825, leaving in his library a violent declaration to the effect that he had never *really* believed in the Shakespeare Papers. Montague Talbot achieved some success in a short career as an actor, and before he retired into rural domesticity played Charles Surface at Drury Lane. William used often to talk of the Forgeries, and never ceased to declare his father's innocence and his own sole authorship. He died in Suffolk Place, London, on April 17th, 1835.

He had ridiculed the criticism of his age by exploiting its deepest sensibilities, and the literary world could never really forgive him.

APPENDICES

Appendix One

ANACHRONISM AND BORROWING IN THE FORGED PLAYS

Vortigern and *Henry II* were never printed in their original orthography, and not published until after the collapse of the Forgeries. The plays, like the other Manuscripts, contain numerous anachronisms of style, language and feeling, the latter of which are worth examination for the light they throw on William Ireland's own beliefs, and on the moral and political attitude of his time.

The most noticeable anachronism is religious sentimentality. The characters take every possible occasion, sometimes chosing the most inappropriate moments, to invoke the deity in terms of middle-class piety that are both un-Shakespearian and psychologically impossible. Thus in *Henry II*, Henry, whose furious raging against his enemies has been interrupted by news of Stephen's death, pauses to forgive the dead king with almost Nonconformist charity:

> *"O Stephen, living, thou did'st wrong me much,*
> *Usurping both my crown and dignity;*
> *And in the face of God did'st break that oath,*
> *Which truly to my mother thou did'st swear:*
> *Yet for all this, do I now pity thee,*
> *For thou stand'st 'fore a great, all-piercing judge!*
> *Whose even hand the scale of justice bears,*
> *Whose all-commanding eye fathoms the soul,*
> *Searches e'en to the very thought of sin,*
> *And proves himself at once a mighty God,*
> *Wonderful and incomprehensible!*
> *So then by death, I now do gain a crown,*
> *By death must lose it, is't not so good lord?"*

While the wicked are to be pitied in their death, the good are assured of salvation, and in their dying words forgive those who murder them:

> *"Oh, I die! sweet Heaven receive my soul!*
> *Forgive, oh pardon this his crime!*
> *I come! bliss! bliss! is my reward for ever,"*

cries Constantius as the assassains stab him. Even the cruel Vortigern himself

233

knows the destination of his victims, referring to the "crown immortal" they will obtain when he has usurped their earthly diadem. Religious feelings are not confined to the nobler characters, but shown even by the basest:

> *"Twould have disgraced the name of Murderer"*

remarks one of Vortigern's thugs after hearing the unsuspecting old king say his evening prayers,

> *"Had we to cold death sent him unprepar'd.*
> *For e'en the rigid law itself allows*
> *To crimes most daring, most atrocious,*
> *A time to pray, a time to ask for mercy."*

It is significant that in the play of *Vortigern* alone there are almost thirty invocations to Heaven and the Almighty.

Equally anachronistic are the democratic sentiments found in both the tragedies. Vortigern's un-Elizabethan deference to "the voice o' the people" has already been quoted, while Aurelius, in a passage that was omitted from the acted script, gives full expression to the liberal anti-Imperialism of the late eighteenth century:

> *"O God! why shou'd I, a mere speck on earth,*
> *Tear thousands from their wives, children, and homes!*
> *O! wherefore from this transitory sleep,*
> *That now doth steal from them their inward cares,*
> *Should I send thousands to cold dreary death?*
> *'Tis true I am a King, and what of that?*
> *Is not life dear to them as 'tis to me? . . ."*

Considering the repute of his model, William made remarkably few direct borrowings. The plots of the plays, especially of *Vortigern*, were taken directly from Shakespeare, and the originals of Edmunda's madness, Flavia's wanderings in the forest, or the aged Constantius' division of his kingdom are not difficult to detect. William was forced to adopt Shakespearian situations because none other would fit into a Shakespearian framework; but for poetry and language he relied chiefly upon his own imagination. Occasionally we notice obvious parallels: "Now woe indeed has made her masterpiece," "Good night, sweet, good night," and "Wherefore dost tremble thus, paper-fac'd knave!," are easy enough to identify, but considering the youth of the forger and the speed at which he worked, such echoes are surprisingly infrequent. In a sense, of course, the whole of the verse is derivative, but it would be a considerable achievement to imitate Shake-spearian blank verse without repeating the almost exhaustive imagery of the poet himself. It is to William's credit that he succeeded so far as he did in expressing his own personality.

Appendix Two

THE "CONFESSIONS"

In spite of the pirating of a number of copies, the *Authentic Account* soon became extremely scarce, and within a few years the pamphlet, originally published at a shilling, was fetching a guinea at public auction. In 1805 William decided to take advantage of this unusual demand for his work, and republished his confession in a greatly expanded form, under the title of "*The Confessions of William-Henry Ireland, containing the Particulars of his Fabrication of the Shakespeare Manuscripts; together with Anecdotes and Opinions (hitherto unpublished) of many distinguished Persons in the Literary, Political, and Theatrical World.*"

The *Confessions* are highly entertaining reading, and, as the only complete narrative of the business, have been widely accepted as a reliable, if not final, account of the Ireland Shakespeare forgeries. Unfortunately, however, William was not primarily concerned to "let Truth find its Basis"; his principal intentions were to display his own talents, clear his father's reputation, and score off his enemies. On the fly-leaf of his own copy Malone wrote: "there is as much *falsehood* in this Rogue's *Account* of his impudent Forgery, as there was in the Forgery itself; for scarcely a single circumstance is represented truly in all its points," and although this is an unfair generalisation, it is true that literary historians who quote the *Confessions* as a serious authority may be led into a good many errors.

William's inaccuracies are of two kinds; quite genuine errors due to forgetfulness and an unsystematic mind, and deliberate falsifications made with some interested purpose or to clothe an undignified fact in appropriate fantasy. Of the first kind of error there are few examples enough. William, describing from a guide book rather than from memory, makes several mistakes in his account of Stratford Church, he is unreliable as to the time and circumstances in which individual forgeries were produced, he misspells proper names, and, in fact, makes the usual mistakes of a writer without proper references. But in general he is reasonably careful over detail, and may be taken as substantially correct when he writes as an impersonal reporter.

The second kind of inaccuracy is a great deal more serious. The *Confessions* were written as a personal apologia, and where his romantic vanity was concerned William had not the least feeling for absolute truth. At heart he regarded the Forgeries not as the amusing deceit of a clever young man, but as the somewhat unorthodox self-expression of a remarkable genius, and he had no compunction in omitting or glossing over undignified or discreditable circumstances. His most serious falsification is the omission of Mr. H. It is true that he mentions him as the explanation he gave of the first discovery, and describes the committee set up to enquire into his identity. But of the correspondence with Samuel, the wild tales of the curricle and the country house, and indeed of all such extravagances, he makes no mention at all. In the course of the book he quotes numerous specimens of his own verse, which he alleges were composed at the time of the Forgeries. Actually, some of them were not written until long afterwards, and those that do in fact date from the period have been extensively altered and rewritten, in spite of a direct statement to the contrary. Not unnaturally, William says nothing of his poverty after his flight from home, though it would have been a courtesy to acknowledge the financial and other support he received from several of Samuel's friends. But for a genius to accept help was somehow unworthy; Chatterton had starved alone, and so, he implied, would he.

The direct, controvertible, errors of the *Confessions* are not very many in number, but their cumulative effect is sufficient to change the whole tone of the story and take away much of its value as an objective account of the Forgeries. The book, incidentally, gives an excellent sketch of William's character, but it was written, as he admits in the Preface, "in the anxious hope that nothing herein contained may tend to my detriment in the estimation of the public at large." When he went on to say, "I shall conclude these prefatory lines . . . with a sanguine hope that my conduct will henceforth be regarded rather as that of an unthinking and impetuous boy than of a sordid and avaricious fabricator instigated by the mean desire of securing pecuniary emoluments," he was speaking, as usual, rather less than the truth.

Appendix Three

THE WOMAN WITH RED HAIR

In May, 1796, Mr. Ireland was surprised by a visit from a curious claimant to ownership of the Shakespeare Papers. The incident seems odd enough to be worth repetition in Samuel's own words:

"Saturday evening at Dusk the Servt. came up and said a Lady was in a coach at the door and wished to see me. I went down, and saw in the coach a fat elderly woman, who asked if my name was Ireland, to which I replied in the affirmative. She then asked if I was not possessed of some Shakespeare papers that had made so much noise in the world—to which I replied as before. I then asked her her reason for asking these questions, to which she said 'the best in the world,' for that they were all hers.

I then requested her to walk in, which she did, and then I asked her how the papers came into her possession. She said they had been stolen from her, and that they were hers beyond a doubt, for that she had written them all and that there was a great deal of religion in them—to which I made no reply but requested to know where she lived and her name; she said she lived at Chester, and her name was Austin. At that instant it struck me that I had seen her before, and that about two years ago, when Mr. Talbot called on me and asked me if I would go with him to see a curious character in Newman St. who had seen two moons—and had sworn to seeing men and horses galloping over them; this she saw going over London Bridge and called to a boy to witness it. This nonsense appeared in the News Papers, and having been much talked of, induced me to walk with him, when I found her an ignorant, uninformed woman, but full of the wonderful—in so much that I hurried Talbot out of the house as soon as I could, and returned home. Desirous of getting rid of her, I told her that if she had anything to say on the subject of the Papers, she must go down to Mr. Albany Wallis, my Solicitor, in the neighbourhood, and relate it to him, but I have heard nothing further on the subject."

Montague Talbot confirmed Samuel's recollection, and describes the visionary as "a tall, fat, fair woman with red hair or auburn, between 50 and 60, and with a cast in her sight." Nothing more was heard of her, and William, whom his father questioned in the hope that she might be related to Mr. H., could give no information.

BIBLIOGRAPHY

MANUSCRIPTS

The collection in the Additional Manuscripts at the British Museum.

Letters from several collections in the Bodleian Library, Oxford.

An annotated collection of William Ireland's Forgeries, in the possession of Mr. H. Harvey Frost.

CONTROVERSIAL WORKS PUBLISHED AT OR NEAR THE TIME OF THE FORGERIES

ANON. *Precious Relics, or the Tragedy of Vortigern Rehears'd.* 1796.

ANTENOR. *A Letter to George Chalmers.* 1798.

BATE-DUDLEY, HENRY. *The Great Literary Trial . . . of Vortigern and Rowena.* 1795.

BOADEN, JAMES. *A Letter to George Steevens.* 1796.

CHALMERS, GEORGE. *An Apology for the Believers.* 1797.

CHALMERS, GEORGE. *A Supplemental Apology for the Believers.* 1799.

IRELAND, SAMUEL. *An Investigation of Mr. Malone's Claim to the Character of a Scholar.* 1798.

IRELAND, SAMUEL. *Mr. Ireland's Vindication of his Conduct.* 1796.

IRELAND, SAMUEL. *Vortigern* (Introduction). 1799.

IRELAND, SAMUEL. *Henry II* (Introduction). 1799.

IRELAND, SAMUEL. *Miscellaneous Papers . . .* (Introduction). 1796.

IRELAND, W. H. *Authentic Account of the Shakespearian MSS.* 1796.

IRELAND, W. H. *Confessions.* 1805.

IRELAND, W. H. *Vortigern* (Introduction). 1832.

MALONE, EDMUND. *An Inquiry into the Authenticity of Certain MSS.* 1796.

OULTON, W. C. *Vortigern under Consideration.* 1796.

OWEN, G. *Chalmeriana.* 1800.

PHILALETHES. (See Webb, F.).

WALDRON, F. G. *Free Reflections.* 1796.

WEBB, F. *Shakespeare's MSS. Examined.* 1796.

WYATT, J. *A Comparative Review of the Opinions of Mr. James Boaden.* 1796.

OTHER SOURCES OF DIRECT REFERENCE

A Catalogue of Samuel Ireland's Books and Curiosities sold at Sothebys, May 7th, 1801.

DORAN, DR. *Annals of the English Stage.*

LATHAM, DR. JOHN. *Facts and Opinions Concerning Diabetes.*

WALPOLE, HORACE. *Letters.*

The Dictionary of National Biography. Many entries.

The Morning Herald, The Observer, The Oracle, The True Briton, etc., etc. *Frazer's Magazine, The Gentleman's Magazine,* etc.

INDEX